# Nothing
# WASTED

## LESSONS LEARNED
## ALONG MY JOURNEY

# Nothing
# WASTED

## LESSONS LEARNED
## ALONG MY JOURNEY

### Vanessa Guest

XULON PRESS

Xulon Press
2301 Lucien Way #415
Maitland, FL 32751
407.339.4217
www.xulonpress.com

Paperback ISBN-13: 978-1-6628-1433-4
Ebook ISBN-13: 978-1-6628-1434-1

*This book is dedicated to God,*
*and the crew He used to mold and make me:*

*Catherine Guess*

*Susie Watson*

*Plenty Watson*

*William Green*

*John L. Guest, Sr.*

*Vera L. Guest*

***THANK YOU!***

# TABLE OF CONTENTS

# PREFACE

---

**-What is it about twilight?**

---

• **Twilight is the period in the evening during which this light prevails (wisdom).**

---

S ome would say, that life is a lot like the rising and setting of the sun or even the passing of a day. The Bible says with God, "one day is as a thousand years" [2 Peter 3:8 HCSB]. With any day, there is always a sunrise, morning, noon, afternoon, evening, twilight, and night.

Sunrise always serves to give us new hope for the day to come. Morning serves as the buildup for the day, noon is the zenith (the high point), afternoon often represents a settling of the day, and then, there is twilight.

There is something special about twilight.

It's the time of day where the day meets the night. The time of day that is perfect for reflection because whatever has taken place in the day, has already occurred and been set into motion whether good or bad. What more can we do once we've made our day's choices?

In twilight, in that gap where day meets night, one has a unique opportunity to reflect on the day; to see where things went well or and where they went wrong , and if you're blessed, gain knowledge and wisdom, that we could not see through the glare of the sun at sunrise or noonday.

I believe our life cycle works in the same way. In the sunrise of our lives, we are born and spend the morning of our lives, being nurtured [or not] into growth physically, mentally, spiritually, and emotionally. The morning of our lives is where we discover who we are; it is those formative experiences that shape who we will be in the **noon** and **afternoon** seasons of our lives.

In the noon and afternoon seasons of our lives is where we thrive! Interestingly enough, what we thrive in often depends on how we were nurtured in the morning of our lives. If one is nurtured in the negative, oftentimes that negativity is what manifests in the noon and afternoon season. The same is also true if one is nurtured in the positive, more times than not, the positive prevails.

The *twilight* season of our lives does not mean the end of our days! It is a time of our lives that, for most, proves insightful. It's the time where you can look back over the life you've lived and see where the ups and downs were, see where wrong turns were made, and most importantly, have the time to make changes if need be. I'm not saying that one cannot learn great life lessons in the earlier years, but there is something about the wisdom that comes along with age. And while I don't often talk about my age, I am thankful for the wisdom I've attained. Also, there is something to be said for life experiences as well!

Hard living certainly makes for opportunities to gain wisdom in life! However, problem with gaining wisdom through hard living, is your choices may draw you into circumstances that you may not survive, if you are not careful. Hard living can kill you! When you are in the midst of your life, you don't think you are living hard, you are just living.

But what if we can choose the wisdom of others who have been through the same things? What if young people my daughter's age, took a chance and believed that there are people, their parents' age or even older, that went through similar situations and could understand their feelings and still provide them with wisdom to help them avoid potentially serious pitfalls in life?

This is some of what I've considered as I enter the late afternoon of my life. Realize that ***nothing is wasted*** when it comes to our lives! Missteps and mistakes, proactivity, action and reaction—God uses it all to give us wisdom and to place us where He wants us to be. God makes no mistakes!

I think about the wisdom and the lessons that I learned through my own journey and remember some of the lessons my mother tried to teach me. I consider how different I am now than in my youth. Of course, one would expect change, but never in my wildest dreams, did I foresee or even imagine my life as it is today! Even taking pen to paper in this undertaking is a shock. It's one of those lessons we learn along the way, as we can never know where life will take us. We can dream, and, yes, **WE MUST DREAM!** Where would we be without our dreams? That we must do; but how much different my life could have been, if I had known that some of my dreams weren't meant for me, and that it was okay if my dreams changed. Life is all about change and that change can be exciting and beautiful as well as scary and from time to time, **disappointing!**

So, what is this all about?

This is about sharing and caring. I have always had the innate ability to empathize with others, and it's one of the greatest gifts God has blessed me with. However, I will admit that it hasn't always felt like a blessing because I don't like to see anyone suffer. As a minister, coach, and counselor, I have been happy to share the benefit of my wisdom, but mostly God's wisdom straight out of the scriptures. What Solomon said is quite true: "…There is nothing new under the sun" [Ecclesiastes 1:9 HCSB]. We, as humans are not as unique as we think we are! Faces may change, but the problems we face seem to remain the same throughout time and memorial. Greed, lust, loneliness, sadness, integrity and parenting issues, etc. have been a part of human history since biblical times! That's why the Bible is a sound doctrine for our lives because in it we have countless examples of these issues and more.

*Nothing Wasted: Lessons Learned Along My Journey* is admittedly a lot more for me than it may be for you. One of the lessons I've learned along the way, is that when there is something within you that needs to be expressed, then it must be expressed! What good is any wisdom you receive if you cannot share it with someone else for them to benefit from? At the end of the day, this manuscript is to me as the Holy Spirit was to Jeremiah "…Like fire shut up in my bones!" [Jeremiah 20:9]

This maybe one of the problems with the world today: we hold back when we should let go, and we let go when we should be holding back. We must know when to *go*, when to *hold*, and when to *fold*. This is my time to go forward! There were so many times in years prior, where I felt as if it were my time to go , but when people and circumstances got in my way, I couldn't see at the time, that it was my time to *hold*. Sometimes, I forced the issue and tried to make things happen and failed miserably! Ideas and dreams that I thought would go through to fruition *folded* right before my eyes! What I learned is that the death of a dream does not mean the death of your entire being. I've found the old saying to be true, "When God closes one door, He always opens another!"

Nevertheless, our gifts, and even the gifts of wisdom we received from life or others who are wiser than us, are meant to be shared! I believe there is a responsibility, a moral responsibility, that we have toward one another as human beings to boost one another up—in some way, shape, or form, we are our brothers' and our sisters' keepers.

This manuscript has been birthed from some easy and difficult lessons this life of mine has served up. Though I may deeply desire to, I cannot change my past—past choices and past mistakes. Yet nothing is wasted from these experiences-I can only learn from them.

So, my brothers and sisters, I pray that this wisdom transcends cultural and gender lines and provides you with a little wisdom to see you through. I hope that it helps you navigate some of the pitfalls, that seemingly, with each generation, presents itself throughout the ages. Lastly,I pray that you would feel so led to pass on whatever pearls of wisdom you are able to glean.

Let the journey begin.

# MORNING

"Lord, you have searched me and known me! You know when I sit down and when I stand up; understand my thoughts from away. You observe my travels and my rest; you are aware of all my ways. Before a word is on my tongue, you know all about it, Lord. You encircle me; you have placed your hand on me. This wonderous knowledge is beyond me. It is lofty; I am unable to reach it. Where can I go to escape from your Spirit? Where can I flee from your presence? If I go up to heaven, you are there; if I make my bed in Sheol, you are there. If I liv at the eastern horizon or settle at the western limits, even there your hand will lead me; your right hand will hold on to me. If I say, "Surely the darkness will hide me, and the light around me will be night," even the darkness is not dark to you. The night shines like the day; darkness and light are alike to you. For it was you who created my inward parts, you knit me together in my mother's womb. I will praise you because I have been remarkably and wondrously made. Your works are wondrous, and l know this very well."

Psalm 139:1-14
[Holman Christian Standard Bible]

I am the sole girl child of my late parents; I have two brothers, one older, one younger. For a good while, I was the baby. I have wonderful memories of childhood. For many years, I saw nothing but peace and family harmony. I did not have any memories of my parents fighting over anything. My parents loved doing family things, we ate every meal together, we took regular family vacations, and we went on spontaneous outings to the beach and City Island in the summer. As I grew older, it became apparent that as parents, my mother and father were as human as the next person. Where I thought we were perfection as a family unit, sad to say, we were far from it. And Of course, no family is perfect, but the lesson out of this is, that no matter what issues my parents may have had individually or as a couple, they loved their children and made sacrifices to provide a stable childhood for us.

It is the parental love (from whoever filled that role in your life) that is the foundation to rearing well-adjusted people. What I failed to get the true gist of, is that I have a heavenly Father who never failed. He created me and chose the right parents for me. I know that some people have challenging upbringings, and perhaps there are things that you would have changed about your childhood because there are definitely things I would have changed, but our heavenly Father makes no mistakes.

The psalmist David understood this, and in Psalm 139, he describes how God went to work on his life because from the beginning, God knew David, right from the womb.

# GOD SPEAKS TO US FROM THE BEGINNING

I was always told that I did not easily warm up to strangers, or even family members who wanted to hold me. So, my parents characterized me as not being friendly as a baby. But, having a child of my own, I believe that God gifts us as babies, with discernment. I believe, I had innate instincts to discern between those whom I knew and those whom I did not.. It has been said, children should not be forced to be held by anyone whom they initially do not go to. Having a discerning spirit is always an asset in your encounters with others. Interestingly enough, children have a keen instinct and discernment about people, which we seem to lose as we enter adulthood.

As a young child, situations occurred in my life where I lost my ability to discern who should and should not be around me, resulting in loosing my innocence at a young age. I suspect and fear, that young people of this generation, have no idea what childhood innocence is. So much of the world is pushed into their faces through the media, the doorways of our homes and schools, and, at times, the doors of our churches! My heart breaks for so many children and teens of today, who would probably laugh in my face and call me stupid or crazy for believing that children should be raised in innocence and should not be exposed to too much too soon. How unfortunate that it has become the norm for so many children to come up like me, with innocence lost. I'm not just talking about innocence lost through sexual abuse, violation, or assault; I speak of a range of attacks and circumstances that causes a child to grow up without the firm foundation that many of their parents and grandparents had. Times have changed, values have changed and morals have changed. Satan's attacks on the children are masked and come in different forms. This is the age where children are being raised by screens and apps, bombarded with violence and sex on television and the breakdown of the traditional, nuclear family as been normalized to the point where many children are living in single-parent households. All these examples can lead to a loss of childhood innocence.

As a single mother, even though I feel I have done a great job raising my daughter, with God's help and a great support system, I know for a fact that there was a loss of innocence for her . It became apparent when I realized that she was the only one who did not have both parents at school events, or a father who would and should be the first example of how men should treat women. These circumstances have an adverse effect on children, and it should be addressed early and often, so that despite the situation, the child can grow up with a solid sense of self-worth.

Yes, there are so many admirable single mothers out there who have successfully raised their children, but I would venture to say, that we cannot fully admit that we didn't need the father to assist; to do so, would be a lie. God, our Heavenly Father, had the plan for a successful family unit and model for the family life. When unfortunate events take place that mess up that perfect model Christ has set into place we indeed need the Father to intervene, every step of the way!

Psalm 139 is so essential in firming a child's foundation in our world today. With all the ways that innocence can be and is lost, children need the strength and truth of this biblical text to help them grow up confidently.

- **It is imperative that children be taught this crucial biblical fact.**

I just mentioned a few examples of how childhood innocence is demolished, but Psalm 139 is the blueprint, the instruction manual, for children coming up in this world. In this passage, David speaks of God's omniscience and omnipresence—God is all-knowing and everywhere, And because of His knowledge and who He is as Creator, we should never question our Source! We may feel like we can hide who we are, but there is no hiding from God because He was there from the very beginning. God knows everything about us, even to the number of hairs on our heads (Matt. 10:30). God's character goes into every one of His creations. He is our creator, the author of our story. His love is unconditional, meaning He accepts and loves us and is with us through every situation.

Unfortunately, so many children in this generation, do not belief in God, or believe that God has any power or authority due to of their present life circumstances or condition. They need to know, that the Creator that brought them to life, has a specific plan for their lives. That does not mean the life will always be rosy or pretty, but if they can understand that their life didn't just happen, that they were created for a purpose and a plan long before being conceived, then we could raise our children to understand that they will make an impact for good in this world! Children need to understand that God loved them so much in their conception and that same love follows them through life and even now. There are a lot of children that don't get any love from their parents, so they need to know that God, the Father in Heaven is so much more of a mother or father, than any human parents can be.

# PARENTS ARE JUST PEOPLE ON ASSIGNMENT FROM GOD

- **We don't choose our parents, but God does for a purpose.**

Parents!

What can we say about our parents?

Well, the stage of life that I find myself in, definitely will influence my answer to that question.

As a little girl, my parents could do no wrong. Oh, the sun rose and set over my parents! They were awesome! As I said, there were some wonderful times.

But, as children start to develop their own personalities and begin to start thinking more of their own thoughts, they begin seeing their parents as people. It's an incremental process because for a long time, our parents are the providers, so instinctually we look at them as "gods," of sorts because they are doing everything for us . The type of parents a child has—good or otherwise —will determine how early that child begins to notice their parents' faults and frailties. This will change a child's feelings about their parents. Bottom line, our feelings about our parents can run the gamut throughout our lives. However, no matter what we do or how we feel, the choice for parents was not our decision—it was God's.

You might be asking God, "What on earth (or in heaven) were you thinking when you assigned those people to be my parents?"

My relationship with my parents was, at times, complicated; meaning when everything was wonderful, it truly was wonderful! This ties into what I was saying about how as children, we don't have a realistic view of who our parents are. Most people don't look at their parents and wonder what they might have been like as children, typically, we get that information from our grandparents, and it wasn't any different for me I didn't dig deeper into what made my parents tick as children.

As the sole male child of his single mother, my father did not mention much about his childhood This is not to say it was a bad childhood. I discovered some time after he passed, that his mother, my grandmother, and my great-grandmother held down the household which consisted of my grandmother's two younger brothers and two younger sisters and my father. I always felt a special affinity toward both of my maternal and paternal grandmothers, even before I became a single parent. I always felt they were determined women who did what they had to for their families. Which proves my point, that in my case, I never thought to ask what it felt like for my daddy to grow up without knowing his father. All I knew was that he was the best and did the best he could. His wife and children were everything to him, and I guess that's why he did what he did. Even though he had these similar ideals as my mother—also a product of a single-parent household—only by looking through a lens of knowledge and putting two and two together, did I get an understanding of how my father had self-destructive tendencies.

While my mom didn't grow up with her father in the home, she was connected to him and the family he was created with his wife.. I suppose it can be quite difficult for a man or anyone who doesn't have any clue about the other half of himself, and perhaps even more difficult when your extended family isn't as supportive to you as you and your own mother were to them.

My father didn't know that he taught his children about self-sabotage. I've seen it in hindsight in myself and my brothers, but I will speak only for myself. This is the reason why I can pen this work. Despite all the ways I've gotten in the way of a successful life for myself, God used all of it, without my realizing it. That's why I believe nothing is ever wasted and regrets are a useless endeavor. In some ways, this is the motivation for my existence. It's the reason I don't quit, though I've thought about it many times, far too many times than I care to admit. I write this to encourage you, that you are not walking with a permanent rain cloud over your head, but you may be walking around unaware of the damage you are creating in yourself.

Consider this a wake-up call. Look at your life if you keep finding yourself in the same space, then you haven't changed your game plan. Stop, look, and listen. Stop yourself and pay attention. Look at where you are and why. Finally, listen to what's going on in your head, in your body, and in your spirit.

## -Parents really do know best

Parents are not only our first teachers, they are also the standard we use to measure against the Word of God, for better or worse. Sometimes we need to look at our parents and their mistakes, to learn what not to do and what works. We don't always get it in our youth that our parents are less-than-perfect people, like ourselves, with problems and issues of their own. That is why we learn all the good stuff that our parents try to instill in us, and we take the not-so-good stuff and use it as examples of what not to do I had the blessing of having two parents who were raised in the faith of God and the instruction of the scriptures. I don't know where I would be if my parents hadn't made sure I knew God in my head and heart. It was this knowledge, I believe, truly kept me from killing myself through foolish behavior. I believe there is a saying that God watches over babes and fools. Well, I was both at one time or another. If I had no sense of authority beyond my parents, I could have easily run amuck. So often we forget how God kept us through all of our shenanigans and disobedience. Then there are others, who are not exposed to this and sometimes suffer serious circumstances: hitting rock bottom or experiencing a significant loss that eventually leads them in the Lord's direction. Whether your parents directly taught you about God, or you found Him through unfortunate life circumstances, finding God through Jesus Christ is the best thing that can ever happen!

## -God is not to be feared, but revered

Some children grow up, with the notion that God is to be feared for the impending punishment He gives out when they misbehave, but children need to know that God is so much more than that. As a child, I was in need of a clearer picture of who God was.. I grew up fearing God because I didn't know the difference between reverence and fear. I understood *fear* in the pure sense of the word. I listened to sermons at church about the wages of sin and how God punishes the sinful. I took it that God left little room for mistakes. In my immature mind, every time I made a mistake or got into trouble with my parents, God would disown me. I was brutal with myself. Even after I learned that fearing the Lord was to show respect for Him, to honor Him above all else, I took some of that punishing attitude with me into adulthood. As a minister and counselor, I taught, prayed, and ministered to others about God's mercy, compassion, and grace, yet, I somehow didn't minister the same God to myself.

What is the lesson? Well, the Bible says in Proverbs 15:16 [HCSB], "Better a little with the fear of the Lord than great treasure with turmoil." And Ecclesiastes 12:13 [HCSB] says, "When all has been heard conclusion of the matter is: fear God and keep His commands, because this is for all humanity."

*Fear* in the context of these passages references reverence and respect. During my childhood, I remember how certain stores were closed on Sundays, how people went to church in droves and spent time with their families after church. You didn't see many people working on Sundays, other than those establishments that are a open 24/7. There were parents who corrected their children if they said God's name in vain.

Times sure have changed...

Jesus' name and God's name are now used in some of the most disrespectful ways. It's bad enough that I see far more children expressing themselves with curse words, but they also have the nerve to attach Jesus' or God's name to their expressions. Children learn how to do this through their parents. Most parents I know want the best for their children, and like myself, many have sacrificed so much for them. I'm a witness how bringing up a child in the reverence of the Lord can be life changing. Despite being a single mother, my daughter was exposed to the things of the Lord since she was two months old and never saw a day where she was lacking. I know how crucial instilling reverence for the Creator is to a young child; it is truly the foundation for a successful life.

## -Choose reality over fairy tales

It's wonderful to watch children's shows that always teach a life lesson and where everyone has a happy ending, but that is not the world we live in. Teens and many adults tune in to reality television that also portrays a distorted image of real life. Jesus came so that we might have life and have it more abundantly.

I was an avid reader from a young age, and I was addicted to television. Because I liked reading, I tended to do well in school, so after I finished my homework, I watched television for as long as my parents would allow me. So much of what I read and watched on television as a child painted the picture of the happy ending. There was usually a problem to be resolved, someone came in to help solve it, and once the dilemma was over, everyone lived happily ever after.

I think children are very impressionable and life can deal a hand to a child or the family that can leave them reeling. The days are gone where you can raise a child in complete innocence. Devastating losses can take place leaving a child so disillusioned with life. I think the world calls for parents to instill the realities of the world into their children from an early age. I grew up with the view that parents stayed together and loved each other and their children. I thought that since my parents told me I was beautiful, the world and people in the world would see me the same way. I was raised on a "hard work pays off" mentality, that one would be rewarded for their hard work. I learned firsthand how cruel the world can be. I suffered ridicule for my kindness, and have been taken advantage of due to my naïve mentality. Over the years, I had to learn how to develop a "street mentality" in order to survive, something my parents avoided teaching me. Now, I didn't join a gang or anything like that, but I had to learn from people that my mother wanted me to avoid. I had to become "hard" to a certain extent, and learn not to be so trusting of those who were outside of my family. Some people call it developing "street smarts." I had to get smart fast, and yet there were still times I felt like a dummy. My body wasn't injured, but the mind, my self-esteem, took some serious hits over the years—yet, I still survived.

So, when I found myself pregnant, I knew I wanted to shield and protect, but I also had to teach her about the how the world operates. . I knew that no matter how successful I was in my career or what neighborhood I lived in, there was no escaping the mark on African American females in this country. We are the only female group, I know of whose own men tend to turn away from them, and more and more often prefer to marry outside of their race. African American women tend to be objectified and certainly not valued as much as women of other races.

Based on this sad history, I dug in and I shielded my daughter as much as I could. I also had to do some serious teaching along the way, so my daughter wouldn't lose the beauty God gave her in a world that tends to use, hate, and destroy beautiful things. Her beauty is tempered with the realities of this world, which unfortunately started with her father choosing not to be in her life. The reality that because of her gender and race, she will be held back, looked over or thrown to the side. The realities of men wanting to conquer her beauty and count her as a notch on their belt or be threatened by the successes she is bound to achieve. The realities of this world that there are more and more people that don't know God, hate God, or hate those who love Him.! The reality that there are more people in the world willing to hurt you than help you.

I don't mean to paint a hopeless picture. We do live in a world that seems to be hopeless at times, but there is a remnant of people that are opposite of what I described. I'd like to think that "like attracts like," and that she and others like her will find one another and change the world. The biggest reality that we can teach our children is as long as they have breath in their bodies, despite all odds, and their environment, THEY HAVE THE ABILITY TO CHANGE THE WORLD!

# NOON

## ON BEING A MOM

If you'd asked me five years ago what my greatest accomplishment in life was, right off the bat, I would've said giving birth and raising my daughter.

It was a trying time when I found myself pregnant and without the support of my daughter's father. She was the gift that I almost gave away. I'm not writing anything that she doesn't already know. Single motherhood wasn't hard in the context of raising her; it was hard was not having a situation that was the best for her. I admit that as a teen, I hadn't thought much about being a mom. Then there was a period where I imagined that I would have a child, but didn't necessarily want to be married. Then a few years prior to my daughter's birth, I had a desire for marriage. Not in my wildest dreams did I anticipate that I would have a child, outside of the confines of holy matrimony, nevertheless, there was no turning back, so I prayed and promised God that I would give my baby to the Lord, a lot like Hannah did in the Bible. For me and my faith, I entrusted her to be raised in the reverence and fear of the Lord, with a sense that He would be the Father that her natural father wouldn't.

God did not disappoint! I went in all the way with parenting, much in the same way as my parents. I watched every move and made sure I did all I could, so she could have all she needed and God has blessed my daughter. I would say in many ways, God was the mother and father my daughter needed. Motherhood, I admit, is an experience that truly exposes the depth of a woman. Carrying a baby and the birthing process is one thing, but the true trial is in the dedication to the protection, education, and nurturing of a young life. Rearing this child against environmental factors, that at times, try to destroy all that you have instilled in your legacy. Children do indeed give meaning to life. Every moment: first words, first steps, first days of school, school pictures, playdates. these things are just the perks of being a parent. I feel that God gave me an extra portion of blessing when He made my daughter exceptional. Now, this is my book, and as far as I'm concerned, my daughter is exceptional. I'm sure any other parent would feel the same regarding their own child, however, God crafted a path for my daughter, that to this day, has been extraordinary.

When I became pregnant, someone called me a statistic: a young African American woman pregnant out of wedlock. Yet, despite what others wanted to call me, I raised and nurtured a daughter with the gift of song, and God's gift took us both to places I hadn't thought about. I wasn't a welfare mother by any means, but I was single and without her father's assistance. God's grace allowed my daughter and I to visit Asia and several European countries—giving us a completely different worldview than we had before.

Motherhood is an investment that definitely has concrete rewards! You see it each time they graduate: first on their way to high school. I had been told to cherish their high school years because they go so fast, and it's true! I admit that I spent most of my daughter's life completely absorbed with her and her upbringing, that I would oftentimes forget or avoid my own life. However, nothing can compare to that feeling when I watched my daughter walk down the aisle and receive her diploma to watch her perform for the graduate program graduation, and then perform and graduate *cum laude.*

There are so many women who find themselves in a similar position, and I have a few lessons from motherhood to share:

### Cherish the gift and the opportunity of raising and loving your child!

Sometimes children don't come at the most opportune times. No one can plan perfectly for a child because every child is unique. They are wonderful gifts and can be a source of joy if you allow them. Parenting grows you, stretches you, and at least for me, has shown me the depth and capacity of love that I didn't know I had.

### Understand that you are creating the future!

I don't know if people realize what their children are. We are looking at and shaping the future. I know many of us take care of our their families, making sure food is on the table, that clothes are on their backs, and that they are educated. But may I suggest that we also talk to our children, open their eyes to possibilities beyond what they can imagine because we don't know the plans God has for them. We may be raising the next Barak or Michelle Obama, Misty Copeland, Condoleezza Rice, or Jennifer Hudson. It is up to us to instill and to do what we can to grow greatness in our children, so they can take up the mantel and usher the generation after them.

# AFTERNOON

**-If anyone isn't willing to work, he should not eat [2 Thessalonians 3:10, HCSB]**

This is another biblical fact that teaches us the reality that nothing is given to us for free, whether it is physical sustenance or anything you want in life. If one is lazy, you will starve and die.

> "To seek to lead a quiet life, to mind your own business, and to work with your own hands, as we commanded you" (1 Thess. 4:11 HCSB).

I think it's a given that it's always great when one has good role models to follow. I had great role models in my parents and all my grandparents. By no means were any of them workaholics, but they all had the best work ethic. I received from them what I needed to do to survive. It was also good that my parents and grandparents were not prone to engage in illegal activities. Working hard at the wrong things can land you fired, in jail, or dead.

No, my parents and grandparents brought good ole Southern values and their Christian faith up North to make a better life for themselves and their families. They only knew how to make an honest living; they didn't look for shortcuts, and they did an honest day's work for honest pay. This is what was ingrained in them, and those values were passed down to my brothers and me.

I watched my older brother get his first job through the Summer Youth Employment Program [SYEP] in New York City, and took pride in enjoying the fruits of his labor. I couldn't wait to get my first job as well, I don't think I necessarily knew the importance of being willing to work for what you have, but I did know that I always liked to have money.

I got my first job at the same summer camp as my older brother. I enjoyed working, iit made me feel a little more grown-up than I had been before. I got to boss around younger kids who looked up to me as if I were a real adult and I was finally able to make my own money.

Now my parents and other family members always gave us money, whether during the holidays or when we asked, but having my own paycheck was **so awesome**. Unlike others who spent their money on the latest clothes, sneakers, movies, or records, I saved mine.

What I didn't realize back then was that I enjoyed the options that having money provided. It was a concept that I had forgotten until I had very little money coming in, later in life.

Sometimes we learn lessons without even realizing it! The lesson here was to learn the value of money early and start saving it as soon as possible! Even though I enjoyed making money, money never ruled me, and while money was important then and now, I value things in life that money can't buy - always have, always will.

## IT'S OKAY TO DREAM—DREAMS ARE GOALS NOT YET REALIZED

- **You don't know if you can achieve something, unless you get it out of your head and attempt to manifest it in the world**

I googled the word *dreams*, and several definitions came up. One definition described *dreams* as "stories and images that our minds create while we sleep." I would venture to say that this also happens when we are awake. Sigmund Freud has said that "dreams are the window into our unconsciousness." This rings true to me. For so many, the birth of our goals and the realization of things we hope for in life are created and first visualized in our dreams. What an awesome gift God has given to us in the ability to dream dreams. Dreams are important to God, and we know this because in the Bible there are so many things written about people who were inspired by God through dreams. Joel 2:28 [HCSB] says, "After this I will pour out My Spirit on all humanity; then your sons and daughters will prophesy, your old men will dream dreams, your young men will see visions."

Biblically, dreams were mostly about what God had in mind for His people to see about their own future or the future of the people.

So, my personal definition for dreams are that dreams are goals not yet realized. Dreams are the visions, the images of the seeds of possibility for the dreamer. The inspiration comes from God, and it starts with a dream. The dream comes from the mind. Proverbs 23:7[HCSB] says, "For it's like someone calculating inwardly. Eat and drink, he says to you, but his heart is not with you."

When God plants a dream in our hearts and minds, somehow, we seem compelled to pursue it. These dreams are the power behind the future vision, and they help us set the goals that we pursue to create change in the world! You won't know what you can achieve until the dream is translated into an actionable goal. For some, dreams are not supported or encouraged. For others, they have family and people in their lives that foster their dreams and endorse that person's efforts to make their dreams a reality.

What has God put into your spirit to bring to fruition? Is it an invention to help bring positive change to society? Is it a cure for cancer? We are the vessels of God's greatness, and He is able to use us to manifest that greatness in the world! Look at all the people who have brought their dreams into reality, for the good of all. God's word is true when it says, "With God all things are possible!" (Matt. 19:26 HCSB). The question becomes, will you take a chance on your own dreams? Langston Hughes's poem called "Harlem" gives us a glimpse of what could happen to unfulfilled dreams:

*What happens to a dream deferred?*

*Does it dry up*
*like a raisin in the sun?*
*Or fester like a sore—*
*And then run?*
*Does it stink like rotten meat?*
*Or crust and sugar over—*
*like a syrupy sweet?*

*Maybe it just sags*
*like a heavy load.*

*Or does it explode?*

**LANGSTON HUGHES**
**(Rampersad & Roessel, 1994)**

One thing I've learned over the years is that daring to dream is just some of what gives us life! Do you think you can go through life not living a full life because you are afraid to put action into your dreams? What do you need to make your dreams come to life? What are you willing to do for those dreams? Are you willing to commit time, attention, physical, emotional, and spiritual energy to this dream?

As a practical matter, dream fulfillment happens much like how a child learns to walk, one step at a time.

Not everyone has the resources or the stamina to jump headfirst all the way into bringing their dream into fruition and that's okay. I recently made a Facebook post, "If you aren't willing to enjoy the journey, don't take the trip." This admittedly was more for me than anyone else. I made this comment after spending the day before feeling miserable about my life. At that time, I was in the midst of my internship on my journey to becoming a mental health counselor. It was a long-awaited moment that had finally arrived, and I was sleep-deprived, lonely, and socially isolated. I wasn't happy about my internship assignment at first, but God worked it out that I would get an internship not only near my day job, but also near the school where I was completing the graduate program. On top of that, the internship had plentiful and flexible hours that guaranteed my completion on time to graduate. God allowed it to be the only facility who had space to accept me. It was the ideal situation for me, yet I had to deal with the hours that needed to be done, the pressures of my day job, and supporting my recently graduated daughter and younger brother, who were both unemployed. My time and money was tight I had no one who could help me, and I was stressed and tired. The stress manifested in my skin, which reverted to pimples and a rash across my forehead. It was just the day before that I prayed to God and asked Him to let my mom and dad come down from heaven and just hold me. I begged God just to come and hold me or send someone. To make a long story short, God did send someone to hold me, and it was just enough to fuel me for another day. Duringthat rejuvenation, I realized that I wasn't doing all I could to enjoy my journey. I focused on the obstacles, and once again had to stop to remember that I was completing one of my passion, counseling. Was it the specific type I wanted? No. But I was doing counseling. God led me on this path, and He did it for a reason. He didn't have to make an opening for me, and I could've still been trying to finish the program, looking for an internship today.

You can be focused on your goals, but God has fashioned the journey for His purpose, and it serves to create humility and appreciation for the gift of your goals. So, go for it, but be willing to enjoy the process.

**-If God is for us, who can be against us?**

- **Many, but God will not allow those sent by the devil to prevail! Remember Job?**

Have you ever heard the biblical expression, "If God is for us, who is against us?" [Rom. 8:31 HCSB]. There are so many haters in the world that would like to see you fail. There are many who may be living to see you fall. Some of our friends are not even aware of what they do. The devil will use anyone to forward his goals of destruction. Remember the book of Job? Job was tried and tested by the devil himself—something God allowed. Sometimes, that is just what happens; tests will be placed in your way, w that is within the limits of what God has ordained for your life. These tests and trials, though, are able to build character, endurance, and faith. I just want to be real: life isn't always rosy, even people who are pillars of the faith will find that life deals out as many bad hands as good ones. But do you want to know the best part of this? The verse from Romans 8:31 is an absolutely true statement. God is for us and in the proper context in the Bible, it means that God is and always has been for us.. He will not allow the devil to prevail. He is our covering of protection in this life. I have witnessed God at work when it seemed like the devil and his army were seemingly on all sides. I have been struck down at times; I have felt lonely and alone and wondered where my resources were going to come from, but I am a testimony of how God has shown up in my tribulations. There is something to be said for the power of faith which is a life lesson that blessed me over and over again, you may be someone who doesn't call on the Lord in times of trouble, but my hope is that my story will give you a glimpse of what's possible with God. One day you may find yourself in a space where the only one who will stand with you is God!

**-Sometimes it's an attack of the enemy, sometimes it's just a test...**

- **Remember Job? Attack or test, we must return to our foundation and build upon it**

I mentioned Job previously. In the Bible, Job went through some devastating trials in his life. When Satan came before God after going to and from the earth seeking out whom he could devour, God offered Job as consideration for Satan. God allowed Satan to test Job's faithfulness, and Satan took away Job's family and possessions, and his wife and friends turned their backs on him. Job showed himself faithful in that he didn't turn away from God, and he was restored by God.

I give this biblical example because as a believer, I understand that adversity sometimes comes in a number of ways. God allows this for growth. Sometimes adversity comes by way of the enemy. I don't know if you, as you read this, believe that Satan really exists. But you need to understand that there are forces at work in the world that seek to counteract good, and that is called *evil*. One cannot believe in one without acknowledging the existence of the other. Both good and evil exist and interact with our world. There are times when evil, according to my faith, steps in and tries to interfere with the good in my life. The enemy tries to stymie the plans God has for our lives, the divine purpose we are called to, but in God's word tells us, "You planned evil against me; God planned it for good" [Gen. 50:20 HCSB].

So even when Satan puts up obstacles or orchestrates tragedies in our lives, God can make momentum out of the mess. He can make triumphs out of tragedies. Often it takes quite a bit to recognize His work when we are in the midst of madness, however, how we choose to react really determines our end result. The saying is true, *your attitude determines your altitude.* How high (or far) you are able to go depends on your perspective, Believe that God is on your side. Why else did He create you? Yes, a few in this world have turned themselves over to evil and work for the enemy's purposes, but by and large, people were created for high purposes, to shine a light on how great a Creator we have. We do this by living out what we are called to. There are not any promises that life and the endeavors we pursue won't happen without a problem or complication. When these things happen, it definitely can be discouraging and make you stop and rethink what you're doing. This is not necessarily a bad thing. Remember, God can turn situations around for the better. He can interrupt patterns that may no longer suit us, to get us on the right track. Understanding that problems and complications can arise in life gives us a healthy perspective. Life would be quite boring if everything went well all the time. It's what we say we want, but I contend that we lose our appreciation for life if we aren't challenged. Iron sharpens iron, and pressure and friction transform coal into diamonds, it's a miraculous thing. Trials can be considered a blessing because they serve to make us stronger; they help us see what we are truly made of. They strengthen our resolve, grow and refine us like fire.

This is not something I learned early on in life. When problems or obstacles came my way, I didn't embrace them positively. I actually felt like the world was against me—a very immature way to look at challenges that have to be faced. It took wisdom and time to understand this.

This is why I am so eager to pass wisdom on to others. Some things, one can only learn through time. But for other things, such as how to look at problems with a proper perspective, sometimes it's best to get help and advice from someone who's experienced what you've gone through and has made it to the other side.

So, what do you do when a bunch of challenges surface as you are on a direct path to your dreams? You have to examine what's going on. No matter where these challenges derived, test or not, look at the problem and see what can be learned from it and or the experience itself.

# RELATIONSHIPS

**-It's true what has been said, people show you who they are**

- **This saying should be internalized and memorized to help one navigate their relationship life**

Relationships...

Relationships are a big part of life. There are very few people who are able to get through life without being in some sort of relationship with someone else. A relationship is defined as, *"The state of being related or interrelated, the relation connecting or binding participants in a relationship, a type of kinship."*

I approach this topic with a lot of experience, both clinical and life. However, as I type these words, I wonder if I am truly qualified. Relationships are not easy; they are time-consuming and require a lot of work, work that some are not interested in doing. I don't think the world values interpersonal relationships as much as it used to. There has been a definite shift in how people relate to one another. Where visits, telephone calls, and heartfelt letters were once the top means to engage and relate to one another, one now finds texts, snaps, and emails the new norm. Seemingly, the more distant, the better.

With the preferred modes of communication creating such a disconnect, when people either tell you or show you who they are, it is important that you pay close attention. Remember, there is a shift in dynamic that the world has gone through. Digital and internet usage has made it more difficult to get to know others because layers have been ingrained into our lifestyles that make it difficult to recognize cues as to who others are. Texts are not the best way to convey love, care, and concern between two people, and it certainly isn't the ideal way to determine if someone is giving you their "rep" or their real selves.

That's not just the romantic type of relationships, unfortunately, I've noticed that even in familial relationships, at a distance and even in close proximity, relationships cannot necessarily stand on blood alone. We expect that, one family member who always made all the calls to all the family members to maintain the relationships between the households. But what happens when that beloved family member passes away? Friends, we have to do better, particularly my fellow African American families. We must keep our bonds intact. We have the family love that we have because those before us didn't lose track of or didn't stop the lines of communication or the love from flowing. In our distant past, it was the separation of families that was perpetuated in slavery; we must make sure that we stay aware of not falling back into that mindset. We must break those chains and remember our rich culture, where our families contained, loved, celebrated, and consisted of not just the nuclear family, but our extended families as well. It doesn't matter how many friends you think you have, there is nothing like your own, there is nothing like family.

## -You change you, but not others

- **We can be catalysts for change by our words, actions or associations, but ultimately, we are powerless to change other people**

When you have relationships, romantic or otherwise, you interact with other individuals, who are different from you. Sometimes those differences can bring heartache and conflict. What a boring world it would be if we were all the same. In the relationship realm, we are called to interact with different people, including family members. God makes life interesting that way. I love that I am unique in my own way. At different times in my life, I've tried to conform to others or particular circles, but I have enjoyed my differences from others, and at this stage of life, I celebrate and appreciate those differences all the more. This is because I am not the same person as I was in the morning of my life. I have the same essence, that is me, but I've evolved. The evolution, was necessary for survival, but mostly it was a part of my becoming. I think that is a fact for everyone: anyone well-adjusted, perhaps without major mental health or developmental issues, is always becoming—evolving. What that evolution result is, is determined by so many life factors. What I'm saying is, someone who started out as being positive, over time could become quite negative, all because of mitigating factors. This brings me to the subject of change.

*Change* according to Merriam-Webster.com is *"to make different in some particular : to make radically different : **transform** : to give a different position, course, or direction to : to replace with another : to make a shift from one to another : **switch** : to undergo a modification of : to become different."*

I do believe that we are becoming, for better or worse, however, I do believe that the path we take has a lot to do with our choices. There will be circumstances outside of our control, but what we do with that, how we respond to those circumstances, is totally up to us, and in that we form paths that shape our lives.

We have to make the decision: will life change us, or will we change our lives?

That's the decision we all have to make. The product of that decision is who you meet in the mirror every day and who you meet when you walk out the door and how you interact with others. It is the decision that we all must make on our own, and that is why, my friends, we cannot change people, we can only change ourselves.

Ladies, we can't change our men. We can't make them fall in line with our program. We can't make them stop cheating if they are cheaters. We can't make them stop being a slob if they are messy. We can't make them be a romantic type if they aren't one. We cannot change our men.

Fellas, you can't change your lady. You can't make her into a sports lover if she isn't one. You can't stop her from being bossy if she is bossy and the same thing goes regarding other aspects of romantic relationships. You cannot change the person in front of you, the one you sleep next to, the one whom you raise your children with, But you can change the man or woman you meet in the mirror every day. You can change you if you want to.

We can be a catalyst for change. In our relationships with others, our very existence, our way of being and showing up in the world, can be the catalyst for change in others— not you by force, but by you being who you are; your essence. You have a particular influence on people. all the people God has already designed and orchestrated the people for you to have that influence on . With who you are, you can bring about change. Hopefully that change is positive.

What it boils down to is, you cannot change your husband, wife, lover, significant other, or family member, but you can change how you respond to them. You can make the decision to accept the person they are in your life right now, all while you are doing your own evolving. Only God knows what the end result will be; you will either continue to grow into a deeper relationship or grow out. I'm not saying divorce or ending of relationships will necessarily happen, but for some people, it will. Perhaps, for those particular relationships, it won't be a bad thing. We don't have a right to make another person be something else for our benefit. Imagine if someone tried to do that to you? As a believer in Christ, we are called to love others, and not everyone is easy to like or love as they are right now. We aren't called to "fix" anyone; just know that maybe they are not the someone for you—and that's okay too.

# THE RELATIONSHIP WITH YOU

## -Live your life!

This means different things for different people, but if you are not living in line with godly principles, are you truly living?

This can be a sensitive topic; I know it's a bit sensitive for me. I speak as someone who has spent a good portion of my life outside of godly principles, on the edge of godly principles, and in and out of godly principles. But the truth is, **living in the truth of who you've been and where you are now is important!**

I think so many of us live in a way that seems right, based on the media, and based on what our peers think and do. However, if their lifestyle is not in line with God's Word, then for the believer, trust me, you miss something. You know the scriptures say that God allows the sun to rise on the just and unjust. So, it's not like God is going to make everything great for the godly and not so for the ungodly. For certain, people suffer circumstances and consequences for their actions. More importantly, there is a deep inner joy and satisfaction when as a believer, your life pleases your Lord. I'm not talking about being fanatical in any way, but just living out what the scriptures say: living out life knowing that you will not live it perfectly on this side of heaven and leaning on, trusting in, and depending on the Lord to help you to live according to the Word. It's a feeling you can't really describe; it's just different. While what the world calls *living* is often transient, living according to biblical principles gives you a peace that is indescribable.

There was a saying, "How are you living?" It's a question that aims to call you to go deeper to consider the foundations of your life. What have you built your life upon? Not to say you should listen to me and make changes, but so many have gotten so far away from themselves, they may have overlooked or not paid attention to what they built their lives on. Ask me how I know. I lost sight of, and I'd even venture to say, had not even crafted a vision for my life. Don't feel too distraught over this realization. Like myself, you cannot go back and undo what has already been done, but you can in this moment decide to look at where you are right now and craft a vision for life going forward. It is a beautiful thing that God provides us with a life so we can explore options —even past the noonday portion of our lives! It's not too late, , until you are addressed as "the late_____." My friends, don't wait that long!

## -Pay attention to your life

Part of living your life is paying attention to what's going on in and around it (physical, emotional, spiritual, family), and your impact on and contribution to the world.

One lesson I learned that I wish I knew from my youth was to pay attention to your life. Life often calls from within during some distressful times. When disaster strikes, illness, death, it calls us to pay attention.

One important area we ought to pay attention to is our emotional health. I believe that was the first time since I was four or five years old that I took time to think about, pay attention, or acknowledge my emotions or my feelings.

It is said that feelings can be fleeting and are not to be trusted. Well, there is a hint of truth to that as some feelings come and go, however, the ability to feel is God-given, so we cannot discount our feelings either. Yet society, tradition, culture, and family values tend to dictate our feelings and instruct us on what we should have feelings about. Our feelings are very important. They tell us when we need to address something that's hurting us, things that make us feel good, sad, or mad. They are our internal alert system. When we are children, we don't know how to control our feelings. Children, even babies, express all kinds of emotions. In fact, the only way babies can communicate with their parents is through their emotions. As we grow from childhood, we are taught what appropriate feelings are, how we must control our feelings, and even how we should feel certain feelings or suppress them in deference of others. Of course, we should be considerate of others and how they feel, but never to the detriment of our own well-being. Yes! I said it! We should look out for our own feelings because we matter, and at the end of the day, others will not tell you that they are looking out for their own feelings as well. As selfless as one might try to be, or pretend to be, even at the most basic level, people are looking out for their own feelings.

So, what am I saying? Well, one must be very careful to strike a balance in this. If you are someone who suffers from low self-esteem like I once did, it can be very easy to forget about yourself and your feelings. I often felt that what was appropriate was not to ruffle feathers, and I made so many efforts to make others feel good or better about themselves. I often put my feelings on the back burner, even when I felt uncomfortable.

This is not good for anyone. Our feelings matter as much as the next person's. There are instances where it is right to subjugate your feelings for someone else's, but it shouldn't be happening all the time, and it shouldn't be a situation where you are hurting yourself. Consider your feelings and emotional state everyday.

How do you get to know who you are, really, if you don't pay attention to your feelings or emotional well-being? There are more times than not where I didn't check in with myself to see what I was truly feeling. It's almost the equivalent of going through life numb—numb to yourself. That is definitely not a way to live. Some are so unaware of their feelings and the state of their emotional being that when something happens that forces them to stop and take a look, they are taken by surprise and most times unpleasantly. Being in touch with yourself emotionally isn't as deep as it sounds. It is simply spending some time acknowledging what you feel about things that are important to you and figuring out what's not so important, taking time to note what you like, what you don't, and why. It is spending time paying attention to your feelings to determine what you will stand for and what your value system is. The world is full of so many distractions, that I believe people don't even realize that this internal neglect is happening. I believe this is the subtlest neglect of all that we do to ourselves. Our physical health is another area people tend to neglect.

As an African American female in America, I've noted that health is one of the main areas African Americans neglect. African Americans are prime candidates for high blood pressure and hypertension, diabetes, colon cancer, and fibroids. While we may be genetically predisposed to some of these disorders as a race, it has been proven that there are other factors, like diet, that play a role in our people developing these conditions. However, today, there is early prevention screenings that can detect the onset of these illnesses. Why, I wonder, are people still reluctant to go to the doctor? I realize that we are in an age where employers in the United States do not pay for healthcare, but with the Affordable Healthcare Act, care is even more accessible, despite efforts to try to end it.

We must also take into consideration cultural norms regarding this issue. The whole point is that we cannot be afraid or distrustful of the healthcare professionals. You are more important than that. If you don't like one doctor, you should find a different one that you're more comfortable with. Fortunately, this wasn't an issue for my family; we didn't to have to deal with too many illnesses.

Awareness and spending time taking care of the body is the only way one will survive. The Bible says the body is the temple of the Holy Spirit. Yet we often are not very careful about what we put in it and what we do with it. Even more, people fail to realize that there is a connection between our mind and body; disease and dysfunction tend to have an effect on the mind and vice versa. Even sexual intercourse by its very nature should make us more careful about with whom we join. With women and their physical parts designed to be receptors, receiving men into their very bodies, there is a sense that we as women also receive their spirit in us. It becomes disconcerting when we have perhaps laid down with someone who is rotten in his core. Maybe you might recall having a difficult time bouncing back from that relationship, even a bit more emotional scarring. There are studies out there that talk about the spiritual effects, women suffer when they join sexually with a man who spiritually meant no good for her or simply was in it just as a game.

## ROMANCE

### Paying attention to your feelings in relationships

Now let's discuss how one should pay attention to all aspects of one's life, including relationships and your feelings while in them. I would say there have been two men that I felt an imperfect, but genuine love for. Both relationships developed initially out of friendship, as well as unmentioned mutual attraction. Here's the thing about paying attention to your feelings in relationships: there has to be a strong and positive relationship with yourself and if you are a believer, with God first. Perhaps the love shared with these two men would have been stronger, or the relationships could have been stronger or sustained if we as individuals had a better view of who we were at the time. One of the men was marred by childhood experiences, and the other believed he was/is like his father; incapable of sustaining a love-ship with a woman and a poor choice for marital fidelity. And yet, God makes no mistakes in who He brings us to, even if just for a season. Both men, handsome and with qualities I was looking for in a relationship, saw me and were attracted to the one who still struggled at times with esteem issues. While I, saw what they may have perceived as the worst in them, still loved them, flaws and all.

My friends, it seems that my story may resonate with so many out there. Our baggage sometimes makes it impossible to pay attention to our feelings in relationships, or who we desire to be in a relationship with, in a healthy way. I see no other way than to get right with the woman or man you see in the mirror every day! That reflection has to be your "boo" first! Love on yourself, not in a conceited way, that's not healthy, but consider yourself as God considered you in creation. Not better than others, but beautiful, unique, and as worthy as anybody else. Pay attention to how you feel about the Creator of your soul; ask your questions that, certainly, no family member can answer. Sit with God, meditate on His Word, and you will eventually hear the answers you seek. Remember, we were made for God specifically to worship Him. Everything else, relationships with others, are His blessings, not our birthright.

So, what lessons have I learned in these romantic relationships?

And what is the lesson in all of this?

There are a few:

- **Love starts with the Creator of love (1 John 4:8 HCSB). Get to know God, and you will understand what real love is.**

- **Love then begins with yourself. You cannot really love another if you don't see you as God created you. You choose to be a product of negative upbringing or problem parents.**

- If you have real feelings for someone, let that someone know.

- Real feelings don't die; they wait for you to deal with them.

- The love produced from true friendship is as potent and as important as romantic love.

# IF YOU HAVE REAL FEELINGS FOR SOMEONE, LET THAT SOMEONE KNOW!

In my situation, I did not feel secure enough in my beauty to believe that someone like these men would want to be with me. I was **SO** wrong! We were on the same page, and in fact, we had so much more in common than we thought!

The lesson one should take to heart is that while you may not be the definition of beauty for all, there is at least one who can and does appreciate the beauty that is uniquely you. Can you imagine if everyone on the planet understood this in their head and in their heart? There would only be single people by choice because people would have the courage to see themselves as they truly are, and fear of rejection would be non-existent, at least I'd like to think so. What the world needs now and will always need is love. If you are feeling the love, you should tell that person. What a difference you can make in someone's life by just letting them know that they are loved. Once again, whether romantically or platonically, knowing that you are loved is the best feeling in the world. There is nothing like telling someone you love them and hearing from someone you care about that they love you too.

I only just began in the past few years telling my closest friends, friends that I've known since elementary, high school, and college, that I love them! Why, if these people mean so much to me, would I wait so long before I let them know how much they mean to me? Yes, I've shown up in their lives over the years, but it means something to hear the words.

*Because when you say, "I love you," and you truly mean it, there can never be a doubt or question about it.*

### REAL FEELINGS DON'T DIE; THEY WAIT FOR YOU TO DEAL WITH THEM!

There could be many reasons why one would not deal with their feelings. I would guess that either the person is not in touch with their feelings, is in denial of their true feelings, or thinks the feelings have been dealt with.

In my case, I think it was all of the above. To begin with, I think I was in denial. I believed initially that what I felt for these people was superficial, nothing deep, but that couldn't be further from the truth. These were men that I spent a lot of time with, and we felt at ease with one another to share who we truly were. Now, we weren't always in soul-stirring conversations; sometimes we talked about work, politics, or people that we knew who got on our nerves, but that was what was so good about it. Two people being able to be themselves with each other; if that's not love, what is?

Maybe there are unresolved feelings of some kind that you have yet to address. You may not be consciously aware of these feelings. Either way, positive or negative feelings, if not dealt with can blow up at an inopportune time or in an inappropriate way. When you think about your emotional health, working through feelings and issues helps you better understand who you are, your wants, desires, and dreams.

What about you? What unresolved feelings are present in your life? In your relationships? Ignoring these feelings is not a healthy or positive way to deal. What would you do?

***The love produced from true friendship is as potent and as important as romantic love. In fact, it can give birth to romantic love.**

I go through cycles in my life where I am addicted to romance and having romantic love relationships, and what I learned from the experiences was huge. Even in my last romantic relationship, I always considered him a "friend" in a shallow sense of the word, but in the past, he was a friend that I wanted to become a potential romantic love partner. He never knew, but I randomly dreamt about him and I consciously stayed away so I wouldn't express those feelings and my attraction. I don't think there was anything wrong with that, except for the fact that I totally *devalued* what I discovered was a true friendship—**with a lifetime guarantee!** The Bible says in Proverbs 17:17 [HCSB], *"A friend loves at all times, and a brother is born for difficult time."*

Isn't love grand? Think about some of your closest friendships, how powerful the love is between you. For some of you, the strongest relationships you have in your life are the ones from your true friendships. These days romantic relationships are here today and gone tomorrow, which is sad and tragic for so many like me who hope to one day to be in loving married relationship, but nevertheless, it is true.

Where are the true friendships? Find them, cherish and nurture them. Maintaining your true friendships requires almost the same amount of work as your romantic love relationships. I want my romantic love relationship when God says so, but I am so thankful for the strong love I have received from **all** my true friendships. What about you? Are there true friends in your life that you haven't celebrated? These are the people you always take for granted to be there, as they always have been when you needed them. It is so easy for that to happen, and I would guess that if you are a good friend in return, it happens to you as well. In having a balanced life, it is imperative to nurture these friendships as much as you can.

Vow to yourself that despite a busy schedule, you will arrange to get together with these special friends, even if it's every few months. I know from personal experience that if one does not deliberately plan to cultivate these close, personal relationships, years can fly by before you see each other again. It is very possible to lose touch, even in the age of Facebook. There are a couple of people who were in my life before time put a wedge between us, and when I did catch up with them, it was no longer the same. ***Confidants had become strangers.***

My hope is that they know how much I love and appreciate them for seeing the real Vanessa and loving me anyway.

It's funny how God tends to use the people in your life or people interested in being in your life to teach you about yourself.

One of life's most basic lessons that is so hard to accept is you can only change yourself, not someone else.

One thing about being a therapist: you must be willing to shine a light on those areas of your life and personality that are just not pretty. I had done a pretty good job of blaming the failure of past relationships on the people I was involved with and for sure, there was culpability on both sides. I wonder how much less hurt I might I have experienced when these relationships ran their course, had I listened aurally and with my intuition and stopped trying to force my wants on people who clearly, did not want what I wanted.

*We have a word for people who force themselves on others, right?* **Never** in my wildest dreams did I ever think that label would apply to me.

I chose not to beat myself up about this, at least not too much because it is rare that you find someone in the morning or even the afternoon of their lives who is so well-adjusted that they are able to recognize such person-ality and character flaws. I'm not one of them. Why might God allow me to go through all that I've been through to learn these lessons? Maybe at the end of the day, I too am being used to shine light into your dark, not-so-pretty places and hopefully prevent someone from going down an undesirable path that leads to pain and misery.

The other lesson I learned from my experiences with men, was that when you cannot see your value, God brings people into your life to show you who you are. Usually, it's all good, but one of the great things about human inter-action is that we learn about the "ugly" parts of who we are as well. We should realize that finding out the ugly is not a bad thing; it's an opportunity to make necessary changes if we so choose.

How often do you do a self-check in your relationships? Do you simply play the blame game when things go wrong, or do you stop to think about what is happening and try to figure out what is troubling and what the root cause of the issue is? How often are you and your partner willing to put in the work to resolve your issues? Again, we now live in a culture where romantic relationships are not valued and are treated as disposable.

## SEEK GOD'S WISE COUNSEL FIRST!

You can't go wrong with God. You can go to God in prayer with ANYTHING! I personally discovered that there is nothing that God hasn't heard or seen before. The Bible says in Ecclesiastes 1:9 (NKJV), "What has been is what will be, and what has been done is what will be done… *there is nothing new under the sun!*" Your situation and even your feelings have played out before in history with someone else, even when you feel no one could feel or have ever felt what you are experiencing. Because God knows His creation, He knows how we operate and that we sometimes, for varying reasons, will not deal with our feelings. It will feel good just being able to cry out to someone who knows you better than you know yourself. God has answers in His Word and comfort for our hearts.

## *SPEND SOME QUIET ALONE TIME WITH YOU*

If you are constantly distracted by outside distractions, how will you be able to hear what's going on inside? Yes, we all have everyday demands and distractions, however, it is imperative to your mental, emotional, and spiritual life to check in with yourself.

This can be done in a variety of ways. If you have the means to physically get away on a regular basis to recharge and regroup on these levels, that's great, and that's what that time is to be used for. Do not fret if you don't have the time or luxury for this, you have other options at your disposal. There are day trips you can take, long drives, and walks to your favorite parks. Or you can spend time by the sea, which is one of my favorite pastimes to help me center and restore. Whatever works for you, just work it and restore your peace. When I confront what I feel and deal with it, I realize where I stand with those feelings.

# THE PRESENT PERIOD

## My Present Period: Transition

I believe this period of my life began in 2009, and I will say it started on July 25th of that year. I remember distinctly having planned to spend time with my daughter's godparents in Harlem. I don't know who decided to go to this gospel café, there we were, and it was good food, good music, and a good time. I laughed with them about having gone to the doctor and complained about this strange pain in my pinky finger and the doctor told me it was arthritis, the kind associated with growing older. It was a transitional moment because it was the beginning of many changes in my life; not all good, not all bad, but it ushered in this period of transitions that perhaps now is drawing to a close.

From that pain in my pinky finger came months of pain in my ankle and knees I thought was attributed to an anomaly discovered in my ankle. No, on the contrary, the pain was attributed to that and more when I discovered seven months later, after numerous X-rays, blood tests, and consultations with a hematologist and orthopedic surgeon, including a bone marrow biopsy, that I have rheumatoid arthritis. I was glad to finally find out what was wrong with me and spent the next six months, walking with pain and having my daughter dress me at times because putting my fingers together or trying to bend them caused excruciating pain. I dropped thirty pounds in three months because it wasn't initially realized that the medication, I was taking caused a diabetic state in me that raised my sugar levels well above 200. I was a mess, tired and just a mess.

This period of time also ushered in my return to my college sorority after nearly fifteen years of inactivity. I went back after a few years of prodding by a family friend, a Soror, part of my church family, and someone who was maybe one of a few who looked at me and saw more potential in me at a time when I didn't see it in myself. There are actually many who see me, my potential and who God truly made me to be. We often can't see the best in ourselves, but I guess that's why the connection is so important. because if I can't see the good and potential in me, and no one is around to tell me, then I'm lost. This is true even though, as a child of God, I should have known I was valuable, being "fearfully and wonderfully made." but if you are looking for someone outside of you and they don't affirm what you are valuable, and tries to beat you down, or convince you that you are not what God said you are in His Word, and you are vulnerable enough, then you won't see through to the measure that God has set forth in His Word.

So, I returned to women familiar and close enough that they might wonder where I am. I returned because in a conversation with my mom, who was as keenly aware of my singleness, thought it a good idea so I wouldn't grow old all alone. It hasn't been a bad experience; my sorority sisters have no idea that with every meeting they are unsuspecting participants in my social experiment to determine the different approaches I can take to relearn how to be more socially engaging, an art I had perfected in my adolescent and college years that I thought was long forgotten. As it happens, just like riding a bike, it is a skill you never forget, it just needs some practice.

This is a period of time where the hibernation of the vibrancy of my soul has ended. Yes, me as minister, at the beginning and the end of the day, is still a woman, with all the womanly needs, hopes, and dreams that non-preaching women have, and like other women, I struggled and fought to keep it in balance because I discovered that trying to eliminate it from my existence only served to deny who I am, and God didn't call me to do that. Today, I walk as woman-minister and minister-woman, however, I suspect in God's eyes, there is no distinction, for we are all called to minister to one another.

In this present period, it's easier to say what is with very little filter, it's a period in time where I'm a motherless child, a fatherless child, and often feel like there is no cov-erage if I fall—who would really care? At one point in this time, there were people in my life more concerned with money than connection; if I had nothing to offer, there's nothing to talk about. I struggled for relevance, to make an impact, and existence, so I wouldn't be forgotten.

In this present period, I am more aware now than I ever was before, like it says in Psalm 90 [HCSB], I have to number my days . . . Who knows the day or the hour? Not I. I marked the beginning of this period as 2009 as the days were quickly coming to an end in 2015. At rock bottom, having been rejected in ministry early on and duped in my day job, I was at a crossroads. I couldn't go into a future period looking back at this one and find that nothing's changed. No, this had to be a period that catapulted me into another period in which I felt I had learned lessons and reached a few mountaintops.

With any new lessons, for anyone, there comes change.

# LOOKING FOR A CHANGE IN PERSPECTIVE

I prayed to God and asked Him to change my perspective, to change my mind about many things and how I saw them. I wanted to change my perspective because I no longer desired to be unhappy, and happiness is often said to be a choice. Choosing to be happy is not an easy feat. Changing your perspective is also not easy, especially, if you have had a perspective that you have held on to for many years. I think sometimes, if we have experienced so much negativity through others or experienced it through circumstance, where our life has had a few more hard knocks than others, we may subconsciously have a hard time finding the good in life. Life has so many twists and turns, and those downward turns can leave a person down. The basic life lesson is that life consists of peaks and valleys, and like it or not, if one wants to live, we have to ride it out.

I asked God to help me change my mind. I wanted my Heavenly Father to change how others perceived me; to make me more loveable, attractive, and approachable. I hate the loneliness that I feel way too often. I want to allow myself the freedom to be me, while I teach others to do the same. It's interesting that I believe I can coach others, as I struggle to get myself to do the things I need to do, to get to the next level, but I realize that I'm not unique in this. So many can do for others what they have trouble doing for themselves. My problem has been that I kept looking for others to take care of what I needed to take care of myself. That's where so many go wrong. The media, things from outside often dictate what should be done from within. There are some who will never learn this lesson, always having someone around to help pick up the pieces, to make it better, to make it alright,

but I've also learned that these lessons, while taught singularly in me, doesn't mean I have to be in a social vacuum. The Bible says in Philippians 4:13 [HCSB], "I am able to do all things through Christ who strengthens me." If your life calls for change and you've prayed about it, it is possible. If the Lord allows, change can come very quickly. However, most times there is always value in the journey and the process, and that often means it's a day-by-day effort. There is no telling how long; it's different for everyone, but it's definitely worth the effort. Courage to change is not easy. We can get caught up in our habits, in doing certain things, whether positive or negative. Change brings us out of our norm. It brings us out and into something different, into uncharted territory. It may feel like walking out into the middle of the ocean, out into the deep without knowing how to swim. It's like going bungee jumping off of the Grand Canyon unsure if the cord will hold up. It is also important to note, that we cannot judge one another's changes because change and the ability to change is so very personal. So even if the change is deciding to go to work a different way two to three times a week, for the person making the change, it's huge and important.

Again, one of the most challenging things to change is the mind. The more you mature, the more challenging it becomes to do this. Not for lack of desire, but there is a physiological phenomenon in the brain when we do things, and think things repeatedly. It's as if an imprint is formed in the brain. One has to take time to consciously do differently, over and over again, until it becomes one's new pattern; one's new normal. In my life, and perhaps others can benefit from what I did, a change couldn't begin until I was willing to evaluate what got me to where I was at the present. Therapy was part of this process. At first, I was reluctant to go there, but something happens when you get to the brink: when you get to the edge of a cliff and you don't want to fall off, when you are out in the deep of the ocean and desire a life raft—**anything** to pull you back, to save you.

During this period of my life, whenever I saw anything positive and life-affirming, I could grasp onto to bring me back, I went toward it. This was a transitional part of my life, as I finally reached a period of sustained remission with the RA, and my daughter was now in high school growing musically and excelling academically. My mother, who at this point, had enjoyed a lengthy period of remission from cancer, but would soon have to reenter battle, was also in a good place. As a codependent, I found that when all the fires were put out, I couldn't look at what had been brimming in me for many years and had reached a point where I could have succumbed to the flames and been consumed. In reality this was the issue, not being willing to look at me and deal with my own issues. Much better to do so when life is going well. When things are going badly in life, it becomes harder to face this. All of a sudden, I had a couple of setbacks. I was not selected for a ministry position, and the doctors told me my mother would not recover from her cancer diagnosis. Though I held out for hope for my mom, I knew the handwriting was on the wall, and I had to get help so I could deal with the unknown that lay ahead.

I had already decided that despite our differences, I would make my time with my mother count. The differences no longer mattered because I would always love my mother, and I did everything I could to will her back to good health. My time in therapy helped me to understand some things in the dynamics of my relationship with my mom, were still active in my life and affecting my living. Therapy helped me create the change that I needed in my life. After the passing of my mother,I participated in some coaching, which helped me think about and create a vision for my life. Again, not much in the way of sustainable change can occur, if you are not willing to grapple with where you've been and how you've arrived at your present state. Change, as arduous as it can be, also tends to be good for the soul.

# ME IN MINISTRY

## IN THE BEGINNING...
### The Present Period: Me as Minister

There is a fine line between ministry and sexuality or me as a minister and me as a woman.

This present period of time is where the hibernation of my vibrant sexuality ended. At the beginning of the day, yes, I am a minister, but at the end of the day, I am **still a woman**; with all the womanly needs and desires that non-preaching women have. Also, like other women, who struggle to keep their identity, I struggled and fought to keep the balance because I discovered that trying to eliminate it from my existence, only served to deny who I am, <u>**and God didn't call me to do that**</u>.

I think that as a result of my past experiences, past abuse, past everything, I developed a warped sense of view and understanding about love, relationships, and who I am supposed to be. Oftentimes, , your parents, your grandparents, and your entire tribe or village, have established values, and part of being a parent is to pass on those values, to your children. So much of who I am and who my mother really was, was lost to me, until recently. I now have a greater understanding as I looked at her, not just as Mom, but also as a woman in her own experiences; experiences that maybe I didn't pay attention to as a daughter. My mom was raised by her maternal grandparents, and her mother was not in the home because she worked out of state. That's not to say she didn't get the best upbringing,she did,but it was from her grandparents, so she received her grandparents' values, which were in a sense her mother's, but different. My mom didn't get the benefit of her mother's acquired wisdom for the day and age she was growing up in,and that was crucial.

I think with every generation, people take the good of what they have been taught and then naturally pick up what is best for them, and that becomes a part of their value package.

My mother grew up with her grandmother's value package, and from bits and pieces of what my mother told me, her grandparents loved her, but they were strict, and were old-school, for her generation. It is what it is. Their values became ingrained in her because she was with them from age three to eighteen in their home. Where else would she learn her family values?

Even when she attempted to do things for my brothers and me, that were different and easier on us than the way her grandparents had been on her, but it was still a somewhat strict upbringing. I always wondered, in my teenage years, why my mother and I bumped heads and disagreed so much. Well, she had an old-school value system, and it was hard for me as a young person, living in my generation being taught by someone who was three generations behind. There was a disconnect. I thought a lot of what she did, and our expected roles seemed so old-fashioned. Other people's parents seemed hipper and looser, probably because other people's parents weren't raised by their grandparents, but their own mothers and fathers. Not to say my upbringing was bad, just understanding the differences now, in hindsight.

When my mother told me about sex, she told me not to do it until I was married, but I didn't get the why. I also didn't get how beautiful it could be when it's done in a committed, married relationship. This is crucial information for a young person who has peer pressure and sex all around them in their high school years. For a young lady trying to figure out the right thing to do, for someone who was insecure and unsure of her identity, and who wondered if who she was at the core was acceptable to others; not knowing they why was hard to grasp. I got teased a lot at school. I wasn't a popular beauty of the times. Unfortunately, I didn't see my beauty through a clear enough lens to stand up for it, and that caused me a lot of issues. My parents assumed that I saw the beauty they saw in me. I was always praised for my grades and schoolwork, but I don't remember being put in front of the mirror, like I did so often with my own daughter, and having them point out how beautiful I was. That didn't happen because I honestly believe that because I was book smart, my parents assumed I was smart about me.

They didn't know how CLUELESS I was. With a lack of information about sex, good sex and not-so-good sex, I didn't have the best instruction in this area as it relates to Vanessa as a person. For someone who wanted attention, for someone who was looking for love outside of themselves because they weren't taught how to do it within, you did what you could to get it, and that's what I did.

When you have an unclear picture of who you are and all these environmental proponents are around you that can affect your life, it's easy to see something that's a part of you that's alright—that's okay under right circumstances, but it can be twisted if you don't have the information.

I am a sexual being, just like anyone else. I think many of us in society deny our sexuality, or the feeling of wanting sex because of our value package. . When I was a teenager, I denied it because it wasn't socially or biblically acceptable to engage in sexual activity outside of marriage at the time. Certainly, in the values system, the values package that I was given by my parents, I already felt bad about myself because others around didn't accept me. I also had this part of me that socially and morally was against the value system of my family. I didn't want to disappoint them, but, it is what it is; a recipe for self-hatred and low self-esteem.

When I became a minister, I took on the value package of not just what the Bible says, but also the value system of the established denomination that I was born into. Even as a minister, I still failed in my romantic relationships. I still seemed to attract men who didn't fully see me and did not treat me and cherish me in the way that I should have been treated and cherished. The only thing that was different was I was meeting men who claimed to have a relationship with God. I buried my sexuality, I walked around not looking like the beautiful woman that I knew I was. I didn't think about how I looked in my clothes, wore no makeup, and didn't wear a smile on my face. I hid my beautiful smile and stayed away from men for six years. I didn't look for a relationship, and I didn't try to be in one. For those six years, I was actually able to function and the world didn't end because I chose not to be in relationships. At first, it was hard, when I use to see others in a relationship, or happily married, but I redirected my focus to ministry, as I think all believers should do, not just ministers, pastors, and the like. Somehow, I took things to the extreme, which was a common thread to the dysfunction in my life. I believe I am not alone in this, and that many people do the same thing.

Thankfully, God brought me out of that "cave" that I put myself in. The fact of the matter is, the sexuality that I have, I didn't manufacture, that was God. I am vibrant. I am sexy in my own way and that is not a sin, it is what God made me to be. I admit, though, that it's tough finding the balance between being the woman God made me and the minister He called me to be. I think we do ourselves a disservice when we allow people to dictate who we should be. Certainly, I'm not talking about established laws and lawmakers; I'm talking about people who mean well, but maybe are misguided in their assessment of you. This is why it is so important that you spend time getting to know yourself. It's so important to understand all things regarding you, come to an acceptance of who you are, and dictate changes you might feel, are required. This way, you aren't derailed by those well-meaning, misguided folks because you have first consulted the Creator's handbook, the Bible, about who you are, and you have spent time with and know and accept yourself. It's only recently that I decided to stop listening to the people, to the church people—yes, I said it, the church naysayers—and started listening to God. The body I have, God gave me. It's not an ugly body, it's a beautiful body. God means for these things to be. He started out making Adam and Eve to be attractive to each other, particularly after the fall, to reproduce and live on earth as He designed, in light of the sin that changed our entire destiny. Humanity has veered off from God's way, but it still doesn't change what God originally designed, and it hasn't ended. He's made us all beautiful in certain ways and in different ways.

So, now I live in my sexuality. What does that mean? Yeah, do not clutch your pearls! Do not gasp, and do not stand in judgment of me. What it means is what it means. It means I'm a woman, I'm single, I'm going to date, I want to be married, and that has nothing to do with how much I love my God and how I honor God's Word. It also doesn't take away from the great love I have for Him and how strongly I feel about ministry—and that's the key. So, how do I dress? I'm not indecent, I'm certainly not inappropriate; I make sure I'm age appropriate, but <u>if I go out to have a good time with friends or mingle, it doesn't diminish who I am as a minister; it's all a part of the same package</u>. I think that's what the world is looking for from the church today, the honesty to say, "Well, look, this is what God meant for us. The Bible teachings are the standard we strive for, but because of the fall, because of sin, this is what we are dealing with."

It could be anyone saying, "I was married, but we didn't know how to communicate…" or "I had an affair, we broke up, but I still love Jesus." And this is how it is for many ministers, pastors, and layperson alike. It doesn't mean Jesus isn't still using these people as part of the Great Commission, this is the reality, and the world is just looking at us believers to acknowledge the truth. The world needs to look up to something, but what the world really needs to understand is that believers in Christ are not the ones who are to "sit high and look low." We're the ones who should be walking with the ones who don't know who our Savior is, and sharing that information.

If people accept, we should continue to walk with them, teaching them the Word, sharing it with them and teaching them how to share it with others. That's why we were created, to be part of a community and not to be "kings and queens of ministry." **I'm not the one**. Even if God calls me to be a pastor, it doesn't elevate me any more than the new Christian. With Jesus, we are all on a level playing field. The difference between the pastor and the pew, is just a different assignment, that's it. With that in mind, you have to understand that people in ministry, are people; they are multifaceted, **just like anyone else**. How unattractive would it be to attend a church where your pastor or your ministers, never smiled, never laughed, couldn't relate to you on a human level because they didn't' know anything about being earthly good. They came out of the womb saved, sanctified, and preaching. I'm talking about the good things about being human, not just sinning. God has not called us to deny who we are. We are who we are, the good and the bad that shapes us.

So today, I walk as a woman-minister and a minister-woman, however, I suspect in God's eyes, there is no distinction, for we are all called to minister to one another.

Ask yourself, **"Who are you really?"** Are you what others say you should be, or are you what God says in His Word? This is a question that I extend to believers and non-believers alike. If you remain uninformed, there will always be someone trying to tell you who you are. I do want to implore those who are not sure, so check with God first. Psalm 139 tells us that we are "fearfully and wonderfully made!" I think that's a great place to start, and I can guarantee you that there are no untruths with God.

## PERSON IN MINISTRY

*Ministry*, what a wonderful word for us Christians. It is often a word taken for granted, used and maybe sometimes abused, but for many, it is one that seems to make us proud to be Christians. Many will say, what could be better than to be in ministry for the Lord?

God has shown me that as a person in ministry, I carry several distinct and separate roles that carry their own concerns. I am a child of God, a minister of the Gospel, a woman, and a mother in ministry—not just in church, but also in life. Being in ministry goes way beyond my church's edifice; it enters my home, my job, and anywhere and everywhere the Lord leads me to go. Ultimately, I am not only a person in ministry that has many roles. As a child of God, I am created by God as a means to be used by Him to bring His people to Christ. I, the person in ministry, the child of God, have been ordained for such duty through my faith, confession, and belief in God and His Son Jesus Christ and by the power of the Holy Spirit.

# MINISTRY DEFINED

To know what type of impact ministry has on one's life, one must be able to define and comprehend what it means. What exactly is this thing most Christians feel so passionately for? There are many different definitions of ministry. As denoted in Webster's dictionary, *the ministry (n) is the office, duties or functions of a minister; the body of ministers of religion; the period of service or office of a minister or ministry.*

This definition doesn't give much insight into the deeper meaning that the word had during the time of the first-century church.

When we consult God's word, we find that the word *ministry* is used at least twenty times in the New Testament. The Greek word *ministry* is translated from is '*diakoniva*' which has the following definitions:

- Service, ministering, especially of those who execute the commands of others

- Of those who by the command of God, proclaim and promote religion among men

- Of the office of Moses

- Of the office of the apostles and its dministration

- Of the office of prophets, evangelists, elders, etc.

- The ministration of those who render to others the office of Christian affection, especially those who help meet needs by either collecting or distributing charities

- Office of the deacon

- Service of those who prepare and present food.

*The Dictionary of Paul and His Letters*, (edited by Gerald F. Hawthorne, Ralph P. Martin, and Daniel G. Reid, 1996), states that for Paul, ministry included all that the exalted Christ did and is doing through His people for the building of His church.

This involved the proper exercise of gifts for ministry that Christ bestowed upon His people, as well as the ministry of those who had been divinely appointed to establish and nurture churches. Also included are those appointed by human agency (deacons, teachers, etc.) to exercise leadership roles in the church. Churches founded by Paul were made up of individuals each of whom had received gifts of ministry to be exercised for the common good (1 Cor. 12:7, 11). Manifestations of the Spirit were a big part of ministry (1 Cor. 12:4-11): the utterance of wisdom, knowledge, faith, gifts of healing, works of miracles, prophesy, discerning of spirits, etc. In Romans 12:4-8 [HCSB], Paul stresses that believers had different gifts according to the grace given to them, which is why no believer should feel out of place or without a place in the Lord's church. Each person has been made for a specific purpose: to utilize a specific gift.

In the pastoral letters, Paul gives instruction to Timothy and Titus concerning the qualifications of those appointed as bishops; teaching and managing the household of God; [1 Tim. 3:2,5 HCSB] and other appointed leadership.

If we are to look at Paul, the essential elements of his ministry are equipping the saints and preaching the gospel (1 Cor. 1:17). He recognized these were the means by which God had chosen to make Himself known to people (1 Cor. 1:21); this was the power of God for salvation. Paul was under obligation to preach this gospel and faced dire consequences if he didn't.

This is a part of the sense of urgency that I have felt for many years about my own commission, even before God revealed it to me. Once the Lord gets a hold of you, it is truly very hard to turn away, and why would anyone want to?

Paul's evangelistic ministry is described in Romans 15:18-19. His ministry did not cease once he had brought them to initial obedience of faith. He taught, encouraged, and warned so that his converts would reach maturity in Christ (Col. 1:28).

Prayer also was a big part of Paul's ministry. The burden of these prayers was that of intercession that believers might know the hope to which they were called and the greatness of God's power at work in them (Eph. 1:17-19). Another aspect of Paul's ministry was conscious modeling of the life those believers should live (1 Cor. 4:16-17; 1

Cor. 10:32-11:1; Phil. 3:17). Paul's motivation for ministry was driven by a realization of the love of Christ for himself personally and a desire for all humanity (2 Cor. 5:14-15; Gal. 2:20), to see Jesus, and to get saved (1 Thess. 2:19-20; Phil. 2:14-16).

*The Baker Theological Dictionary of the Bible*, (editors: Walter A. Elwell, 2001) breaks down ministry in the Bible by the two testaments, Old and New, and defined *ministry* as "the service of God and His creatures and one essential ministry of Jesus Christ."

## MINISTRY OF THE OLD TESTAMENT

According to Elwell, there are three ministries of the Old Testament: (1) prophetic, (2) priestly, and (3) kingly. All three are essential within the covenantal relation between Israel and Yahweh. Ministry is not just for the individual.

## MINISTRY IN THE NEW TESTAMENT

Jesus fulfills the three ministries of the Old Testament. Christ came to minister (Matt. 20:28) as prophecy fulfilled (Is. 52:13-53:12; Lk. 22:27; Phil. 2:5-8; 1Pet. 2:21-25) and as a king (Rev. 20:11). The Word Incarnate ministered to people in their deepest need. Jesus rules, guides, prays, intercedes, proclaims, teaches, loves, and rejoices for and through His people. The church has been called to do this as a royal priesthood (1 Pet. 2:5,9). Each and every member of the church has a part to play (Rom. 12; 1 Cor. 12) in service to God. We are to be slaves/servants of Jesus Christ (1 Cor. 6:19-20; 1 Pet. 2:18-19). We have a universal duty to Christ in whatever way the Lord has chosen us to serve. We are to be imitators of Jesus Christ.

# THE CALL

Glen Whitlock, who wrote the book, *From Call to Service: The Making of a Minister*, explored several themes of the person in ministry: the theological dimensions within which one is called, the ways in which one is called, the ways in which a person's discipleship and selfhood may be actualized in a particular ministry and the traditional understanding of the ordained ministry and its relation to the study of the nature and mission of the church.

Whitlock indicated in *From Call to Service: The Making of a Minister*, stressed that the role of ministry by nature is personal because it is designed to meet the needs of the people. Having this understanding should help the minister in being objective in their service and prevent him from having distortions from their own personal life, hinder their ability to minister.

Whitlock further posited that ministers require training to use certain tools, such as an understanding of theology in regard to the needs of persons, and an understanding of the Word, the concerns of physical and emotional suffering, and the ability to communicate the ways in which God comes to persons. These tools that Whitlock mentions in his book, I believe can be gleaned from seminary study, but are best received from our guidebook, the Bible.

Whitlock indicates that traditionally the understanding of the ordained ministry is related to the study of the nature and mission of the church. The ministry of all Christians is not merely a human activity apart from the ministry of Christ; not to be identified with Christ's ministry, but not totally separate. The ordained ministry is a functional dimension of Christ's ministry: Christian vocation and occupation. It is God who calls man to discipleship. This call to ministry often is described as a "higher call." It is a discovery of a sense of vocation, resulting in new patterns of obedience to God and giving away to a new sense of mission where the minister will serve in the particular way his obedience can be expressed.

All this is definitely a mouthful. So, what does it mean? For me, I suffered from low self-esteem for many years.

For many years, I wasn't in the right frame of mind to truly understand that God had a plan for my life. I had no clue that I was so important to our Father that He created me for good; that good included getting to know Jesus. Sometimes, people have to go through difficult childhoods, difficult times before they are prepared to be used according to God's will. I would like to think that I have more of an understanding of others who have walked a similar path, or young girls who may be walking that path now. Sometimes it takes years before a person is actually able to "hear" the call of God into service.

It was this call that saved my spiritual life; my entire life. It is a sin not to love oneself; in fact, we are "made in the image of God" Himself. Even so, there are so many people in the body of Christ that will shout, "Praise the

Lord" on Sunday morning, but live lives of self-loathing from Monday through Saturday.

It is at the time of our conversion, when we have a true encounter with Jesus, that we have our first opportunity to hear our call. Once we have heard our "call," life in the world is not all we can have; we also can experience pure unconditional love from God, made possible through the sacrificial offering of Jesus to atone for all our sins. This gift of grace and love comes from God, so that those of us who have accepted Jesus Christ as our Savior by belief and confession (Rom. 10:9-10 HCSB) can't help but feel the love of such an act.

I would not give up my daughter for anyone; who humanly would or could do that? In knowing Jesus, I got to know His love, and God's love, and more than anything, it started to cause me to develop feelings of love for myself. I looked back on my life and remembered all the situations I created on my own, where I put my life at risk, and I wondered why God would bring me through. I have been hurt and abused by men so badly that I wanted to die; I would even cry out and ask God to take me away. But though "weeping endured for many nights joy always came in the morning" (Ps. 30:5 HCSB). It was a process, and in the beginning, I felt God inviting me to know Him, so that is what I did. I started reading the Bible more and more and with purpose. I had been attending Bible study for several years, and it was helpful, but I was not serious about knowing God or perhaps I didn't know how to know Him. This time I was looking for something; it was important. In the months that passed, the Lord led me to attend seminary. I started, and people close to me asked me, "What, are you trying to study to be a minister?" The funny thing is that I gave a vehement "no" and that I just wanted to learn more about God. I started going to church every time there was a service, when possible, and helping out around the church behind the scenes because I truly enjoyed it. Before I knew it, I started to feel unrest. I really thought that I was in line with what God wanted me to do, and I actually was, but God wasn't finished with me yet.

My unrest got progressively worse, and it was around the season of Lent, that I decided I would go on a fast because the spiritual disciplines of fasting and prayer are a good combination for making one's heart and mind open to receive instruction from the Lord. When I started the fast, I knew what the Lord wanted of me, I just did not want to accept responsibility. I could not believe that the Lord would want to use a woman like me for the job He had in mind, but by Easter time, I knew without question that the Lord had called me to preach. It had been confirmed by my pastor that it was of God, when he asked me when I would do my initial sermon. However, it took all of those weeks of Lent to submit my will to God's. Second Peter 1:10-11 states, "Therefore brothers, make every effort to confirm your calling and election, because if you do these things, you will never stumble."

Not only did I not want to accept the responsibility, but I had to be sure this is what God wanted me to do. I had to accept the fact that God had bestowed upon me gifts that were to be used in a greater way in ministry.

I accepted the call and was licensed as a minister of the gospel two months later. The adventure was about to begin.

# THE VOCATION

*"Be diligent to present yourself approved to God, a worker who doesn't need to be ashamed, correctly teaching the word of truth." (2 Tim. 2:15 HCSB)*

*"For we are God's coworkers. You are God's field, God's building." (1 Cor. 3:9 HCSB)*

*"Don't work for the food that perishes, but for the food that lasts for eternal life, which the Son of Man will give you, because God the Father has set His seal of approval on him." (John 6:27 HCSB)*

It is not a surprise that right after my licensing, life got busy. It was already busy while I was working "behind the scenes," but now I had to go to different places with the pastor, prepare to give sermons, learn how to assist the pastor as an associate minister, and study regularly. I was already involved in two other vocations of sorts; I was a single mother of a small child at the time and a woman.

It is at this point that things got a little fuzzy for me. Here I was, a minister of the gospel, which was my second job, after being a mother and working daily at my salaried employer. . There was tension for a woman in a vocation dominated by men, where women weren't being taken seriously and weren't well received in ministry. I couldn't stop being a woman, I am that forever; and I couldn't stop being a mother, that too is a life-long responsibility that I would never give up. Certainly, I am not the traditional woman preacher, by any stretch of the imagination. Because of traditional views, many male ministers, at least in the black Baptist faith at the time, had no use for a woman minister. In fact, many still feel it's unbiblical; many believe that the woman is the cause of the fall of man today and because of the fall, women hold a secondary place in ministry within the church.

I never looked at God as separating man and woman and putting them into categories of "first" or "second" on earth. I have always looked at God as someone not holding preference to gender, but seeing all believers as His children and having an equal part in the work of the gospel and ministry.

In the book, *Beyond the Curse: Woman Called to Ministry*, Aida Besancon Spencer explores the foundations of women in and for ministry. She takes a really close look at the blessings from God before the fall and the curses that happened after that. Spencer illustrates that Adam and Eve shared in the responsibility for the fall of man and that before Eve's deception, she was created as an equal helpmate to Adam in the care of the Garden of Eden (Gen. 2:18-24). Spencer also spends a great deal indicating Jesus's teachings and practices concerning women, Paul's teachings and practices toward women, and examples of women of authority in the Bible. In today's society, the issue of women and their place in the church is somewhat controversial. Some men are evolved, and wholeheartedly support great leadership, whether it comes from a male or female. And then there are still some men who feel very strongly in the negative about women in leadership roles. I know for a fact that some of the older men in my church saw me as the deacon's granddaughter and not as an associate minister who has been given the responsibility to preach the Word, but also to act as leaders in accordance with the responsibility allotted to me by the pastor.

Jesus thought it not robbery to reveal Himself to the woman at the well, knowing that she would effectively evangelize to her people about the Messiah. Jesus thought it not robbery to have Mary come and sit at his feet to receive His teaching and rebuked Martha for not doing the same (Lk. 10:38-42). There is not any instance in the Bible that shows that Jesus considered women as second-class citizens to men or that He felt they needed to be led by men or that they should be silent. It is no accident that it was His women followers that witnessed His death on the cross (Luke 23:44-49). It was also not an accident that upon Jesus' resurrection, He first revealed Himself to a woman first (John. 20:1-18). Some may try to use the scripture in 1 Cor. 14:34-35 to justify women remaining silent however, scholars agree that the text speaks to a situation in that church, and not a global shutdown of women in the church.

It was not until I became a minister that I experienced firsthand some male views on women preachers. Why is it that we cannot remember that there were both men and women present at the day of Pentecost? (Acts 2:1-39) That on that day Peter recited scripture from the prophet Joel (Joel 2:28-29) who said that both men and women would prophesize and dream dreams; showing that the coming of the Holy Spirit would not take the time to discriminate among believers, but bestow upon believers according to the will of God. Functioning as a woman minister in my church has not been as difficult as it could be because my family has had years of involvement in the church. I am respected despite my prior actions in the world. Perhaps the respect comes from people's knowledge of what I went through in the world and how I reached my current destination. In any regard, reality sometimes hits when I traveled to other churches with the pastor and the host pastor didn't want a woman in the pulpit.

It had been a common belief for a long time among some black Baptist ministers, that women preachers should be placed as children's pastors or women's pastors or be put in charge of the hospitality committee. I don't have a problem with that, but certainly, a male minister could and should be considered for the same types of positions. God is not a respecter of persons (Acts 10:34; Gal. 2:6). As far as I'm concerned, it was revealed to me and confirmed that I would be used in counseling women as well as preaching, however, I have found over the years, that men have also been sent to me for godly counsel as well. God has used me mightily in teaching ministry as well. I do it all, as God provides the opportunity, for His glory; nothing is impossible with God.

Again, as a behind-the-scenes worker within the church, there was a lot of work to be done, and it was easy to keep my little girl, by my side while I worked. When I became an associate minister, there was more work and more meetings, more training, workshops, and conventions that I was expected to attend. More often than not, children were not allowed in these meetings, and they weren't always able to sit still. Oftentimes, there were just two or three other women besides me in a sea of men and commonly there is an unspoken rule that even though the female may have been allowed to attend, it was for her to sit quietly and listen.

It was not always easy as a single parent to juggle this side of ministry. I didn't like to burden my mother with the responsibility of caring for my daughter for more than two days a week, yet, at these particular functions, I was able to meet other female ministers with similar interests and challenges. It wasn't an easy juggle, for my daughter, who quickly discovered that she had to share her only parent with the rest of the congregation. Many times, we'd walk into the church at 9:30 a.m. together and not to speak to each other again until after 1:00 p.m. when the service was over. I found that I had to share the mothering responsibilities of my daughter with some of the other ladies in my church, who enjoyed spending time with her. It was quite an adjustment for us both, however, it showed me what it meant to be in the body of Christ, the community of the saints. We are to help each other, build up each other in Christian love. We are to provide for the needs of others who are in need (Acts 4:32-37).

# CHARACTERISTICS OF THE MINISTER

Ministry is not an easy task for male or female. There are characteristics that those who are active in ministry possess or somehow acquire through the day-to-day experience of ministry. There is a need to start with the basics. there should be human wholeness, meaning the individual must be healthy in mind and body. You cannot give what you don't have. There can be and is a lot of stress, so it is important for the individual in ministry, to take care of themselves , by getting regular physical check-ups (1 Cor. 3:16-17) from the doctor and spiritual check-ups from their pastor or spiritual mentor. We sometimes have to bear the spiritual burdens of others, but we also have burdens of our own, so there must be a safe outlet for ministers to utilize. In times like this, the individual in ministry must, without question, have a prayer life. How can any believer function without prayer? Jesus told His disciples, "I tell you the truth, my Father will give you whatever you ask in My name.

Until now you have not asked for anything in my name. Ask and you will receive, and your joy will be complete" (John. 16:23-24).

Prayer changes the ordinary man or woman and makes them extraordinary. It draws us closer to God, conforming us to the image of Christ. It is in prayer that God can seep into our hearts and minds and teach, show, and guide according to His will, those who are seeking to be led by Him. The person in ministry needs prayer not just for him or herself, but also to pray for others. The people who sit in the pews, Sunday after Sunday are hurting from scars that you may not be able to see. Those who request prayer and especially those who don't ask for it are vulnerable. There is a sense of the need for prayer and to do it regularly until the Lord speaks or acts on that individual. The minister should have the ability to comfort (2 Cor. 1:4-6), endure hardness (2 Tim. 2:3), feed the church (John 21:15-17), strengthen the faith of their people (Luke 22:32), teach (2 Tim. 2:2), watch for souls (Heb. 13:17), and have the ability to be affectionate to the people (Phil.1:7). The person in ministry should be blameless (1 Tim. 3:2), devoted (Acts 20:24), gentle (1 Thess. 2:7), holy (Titus 1:8), humble, patient (2 Cor. 6:4), and strong in faith (Rom. 4:20-24).

# THE MINISTER AND HER MASTER

What can I say about my Master and me? For many years I have cut myself off from the only one who has always loved me unconditionally. God my Father, who had designs for me since before my birth, was my shadow, until the day I finally decided to submit myself to Him. I am so pleased with what God has done with my life. I am a living witness that this relationship between the Father and His child is extremely important. Persons in the ministry are supposed to be guided by the Holy Spirit, and the Spirit cannot be tapped into if the relationship between a person and God is not an active one. A growing relationship is based on continual and mutual self-revelation, according to Klaus Issler in his book, *Wasting Time with God: A Christian Spirituality of Friendship with God.* (p. 16)

We must be in a position to continually seek to deepen our relationship with God. I need God to help me with the unseen wounds that I've gotten from the past experiences and in my present. Issler tells us that "God's active participation in our lives can be as rich and rewarding as we might want it to be, to the extent that we are willing to make room for all that God desires to be and to do in our lives." (p.21) God is ready and available to visit us at our most intimate and vulnerable moments; eager and willing to meet all our needs. But this friendship-love relationship between God and me is an active process on both our parts. I believe that the deeper my relationship and interaction with God, the deeper and stronger my human relationships will get. I have learned a lot about love, and God is love (1 John. 4:16). I understand that God is always with me and I remember that my good is what He wants for me. One thing that I believe many believers get frightened of is that God's will, will not grant them their desires. I think God's will is something that prevails in the lives of His believers, and once the individual has become converted, the individual's desires won't be too far off from God's will for that person. What I can say, obedience, faithfulness, submission, and love are components within my relationship with God. I cannot move without Him.

Ministry in and of itself is a process. I am a part of that process, and within that arena, I am in the midst of a process of getting to know and continuing to serve the Creator, God.

Who is the person in ministry? It could be the next-door neighbor or it could be the person sitting next to you on Sunday morning. I am the person in ministry doing the ministry of love, exhibited through the preaching of the gospel, assisting the needs of the pastor, counseling and praying over the members of the congregation, teaching Sunday school, and testifying about how Jesus not only came into my life, but more importantly, how He saved my life! These things are not difficult; many untitled individuals do that behind-the-scenes work daily as well, It is the face of ministry.

# MINISTRY CAN HURT

In 2014, I experienced great hurt in ministry. It was the very first time I felt led to answer the call to pastor. This happened at my family church, family, my origins. I wish there was someone who could have warned me about the dangers of this. Maybe I didn't think it to be an issue, as I had seen a former pastor transition his son into the seat after serving for more than twenty years. Not many have asked me what I went through during those months as a candidate at my own church. When I think about lessons learned along my journey, these insights must be shared.

When I accepted the call to ministry and to preach back in 2001, it was never my intention to become a pastor. I *only* wanted to help. In the few years before my call to ministry, I had an experience on a hayride, chaperoning my daughter's kindergarten trip to a local farm. There was a moment on the hayride; that I was watching my daughter, who was sitting directly across from me, not paying any attention to me. The absolute joy she had in her eyes, and the huge smile, along with the giggles—the way she always seemed to be able to draw others around her, swelled my heart. Obviously happy, but at the same time, woefully aware of the situation I had put her in. This gorgeous, beautiful, good-natured child wouldn't grow up as I had, with two loving parents in her life. Her father wouldn't materialize in her life for another few years, but at that time, I knew it was her father's and my sin that created this situation for her. My daughter didn't deserve that, she deserved so much more! In the light of these emotions on that hayride, I looked toward the sky and I prayed for the Lord to forgive me. Even though God brought the best out of my sin situation (my daughter), the consequences landed not only on me, but on her as well.

This rebirth led to me getting baptized for the second time, as an adult, understanding completely what I was doing and why it had to be done. The first time at age seven, baptism was for my family. This time, it was for Jesus!

My life in Christ seemed to have gotten a renovation. I had attended Bible study for years before my daughter was born, but the study and internalization of God's Word, now was more exciting. I was reading with new eyes. My prayers and prayer time were amazing. I wasn't afraid to pray publicly and privately; I enjoyed the fellowship with the Father as His daughter, and not just as a minister or worker. It is a fellowship I continue to enjoy to this day.

I am a witness to anyone who cares to hear that there is excitement and passion in a life lived for Jesus Christ! I feel this period in my life was the beginning of my love affair with the Lord.

My worship was not as demonstrative as others, but I studied scripture and I prayed like I never had before, for myself and mine, as well as for others. The call to ministry was in me; I engaged in church, in service in ways that I hadn't before. I hosted friends at my house from time to time, and we studied the Bible even outside of the church. Not long thereafter, I had my initial sermon, and for a while served at two churches. I went to every service; wherever the pastor went, so did I. I became a regular at state conventions in the other state where the pastor served, went to local convention functions, and visited numerous other churches, and befriended many pastors as well. I was all in; usually exhausted on Sunday evenings; as I still worked by day, raised my daughter, and by this time was finishing my Master of Divinity. Ministry for a woman in the early 2000s was challenging. It hurt when there were pastors who openly made me feel insignificant because I was a woman. There were pastors who wouldn't allow me near their pulpit, who often called on other male associates for preaching opportunities, while oftentimes months went by without an opportunity. There was even a time when a whole year past and I had not been allowed to preach. There was much going on in my church, and despite my faithfulness, I was often overlooked for opportunities to impart what God had given me from the sacred text. I felt that I struggled in the delivery often because the opportunities were so few and far between. There had even been times where I felt I was in competition with other associates, because it seemed that popularity and other worldly attributes were preferred to the earnest spirit-filled willingness to preach. At times, the mistreatment and disparity were so obvious that it made my mother furious, to the point where she was ready to walk out of our church, and never return. Those were some **hard** days. I stayed in ministry because I knew God had called me. However, I didn't understand the reason why I was continually held back and not allowed to be used by God to serve His people. I had friends in ministry that asked why I stayed there and didn't move on. Simply put, I had not heard God tell me to move on. Ministry is so important to me that I was constantly checking myself: is it my ego at work, what within me needed to be adjusted?

Later, it would happen that my church would have another period of time without a pastor. It had been more than thirty years since the church had a need to begin a search. Initially, the church was insecure, with most of us not having experienced this situation before. Eventually, the officers came together because they knew the church had to survive, they made it work and were willing to step up to the plate. No matter what happened with the previous pastor, he took the time to train us. I remember the numerous training and leadership classes he conducted, requiring ministers and deacons to attend. I remember the first time the deacons had to preach. We had to put all that training into practice at that point. I was the sole remaining associate minister, to a pastor I think by the end, didn't mean any good for me. For my church, I did what I was called to do. I preached when they asked me to preach, I did Bible study when they asked me to. I presided over baptisms, I was present for funerals, I taught Sunday School, I gave the right hand of fellowship, and I did a lot more pastoral counseling. I hadn't been given any title for many of the duties of being an interim pastor.

In late 2013, I struggled with putting in my application for the pastorate. I didn't struggle with the fear of, if I could do it, I knew I could, and I believe that to this day, I struggled with the question of, if I should do it. I wondered how church life would change with me as the pastor of my childhood church.

I believe my church did its best in such trying times. Times were extremely hard for me during this time. My mother's health was declining and church meetings regarding the selection process early on were heated. Some people believed only a man could be a pastor at our church, while others wanted real change. Something happened in the process where the pastor selection committee initially disqualified me and then I became a candidate again. It brought up feelings of inadequacy. I did not have years of experience because doors were closed to me, sometimes in my face, experience other male preachers had freely opened to them. I tried to appeal to the people who knew me, my family, and my evolution into ministry. I thought my church family knew that I didn't play church. I expressed to my church that I wanted to help us get back to basics and to get where God wanted us to be, all with the focus being on God, and not the person sitting in the pulpit.

I was voted out of the final round. Two men remained, and a man was selected. I was so hurt. My church family didn't know how devastating their rejection was to me. I don't think they ever realized how much I gave to God, or in service to them. When I separated from them for a few months, many thought my departure was akin to having a temper tantrum, as a child does when they don't get their way, or that I was being petty, and there were those that didn't understand why I felt hurt. They didn't realize that other candidates who don't make the cut, do not hang around—they move on. My feelings, at that time, were if my own church family couldn't see or appreciate my contribution to ministry, when they had the opportunity, or the faithfulness I had demonstrated, maybe it was time to make a change. At that time, I wasn't sure this was God's way of saying, "Vanessa, move on," or not. Though I had spent just a couple of months away from my childhood church, I remained faithful to the Lord, and I went to the churches of fellow associate ministers. I visited other denominations, like the African Methodist Episcopal (AME) churches, that seem to value female ministers and pastors far more than the denomination I came to faith in. There was a freedom that I appreciated during that time. I had time to be ministered to, without tending to others. I believe I had experienced burnout and saw how the Lord used a negative and unhappy circumstance, to provide healing. I was in a place of spiritual rest as I tended to my mother, who at this point, was rapidly declining.

The lesson learned is that family, even church family, can hurt you, albeit unintentionally, not much difference from our families of origin. During his tenure, I looked to the former pastor for leadership and believed he desired to develop me, like my male counterparts, but somewhere down the line, he didn't see me as someone seeking to serve. My experiences in ministry, opened my eyes to see pastors and other ministers for who and what they truly are, sinners saved by grace—*just like me*. I recognize that so many people, like me, hold preachers and pastors on a very high pedestal. The thing is Jesus walked the earth over two thousand years ago. He is coming back, though we do not know the day or the hour. The apostles He walked with were just like us; working men, imperfect men, doubtful at times, reactive at times, yet all given the power of the Holy Spirit to do great works, all willing to follow the Master. There are no perfect preachers or pastors; all are subject to weaknesses and have character flaws, just like those without a title in ministry.

I was able to get through my pain, because God truly ministered to me; I used my counseling skills on my self. I acknowledged pain not previously expressed. Over time, I reflected on the history of African Americans and the church; I could see how African American men in a traditionally male-dominated space, such as religion would be less likely to make room for females. Pastors and preachers historically were held in high regard and by nature of the function, were leaders. African American males during slavery times in this country had no other occupations that would afford a black man a leadership position. As a woman who grew up with a dad and brothers, I can appreciate it, and yet, it still hurt.

Finally, I think the biggest lesson from this, was the realization that God can make room for anyone willing to step up, and willing to do it in unique ways. I learned that impact for Christ, sharing the Gospel, and helping others, of course, can be done in other spaces, than behind the sacred desk. In fact, there are platforms in other areas of my gifts where God has provided a voice for me to be expressive and share the love and wisdom I've received, in my own lane. I have that freedom, maybe more freedom, than a pastor could ever have to share Christ. I don't know, but if there was a lesson, I would like all African American pastors, friends, and acquaintances to know, is that your female counterparts want as you do, to exercise the calling on their lives. There is **SO** much room for all of us. Remember, everyone is called to particular people and groups of people, the ones that don't respond to you, just may be meant to respond to the way a woman presents Jesus. Ministry is truly for everyone!

# WHO AM I NOW?

W hat I've discovered is that when you experience a significant loss in your life, very little care remains for what others say about you and how you are perceived by the world. Grief has brought out the best and the worst in me.

I was deeply affected by my dad's death in 1997. His suffering had ended, but so had a part of my life as I knew it. It's funny, I rarely see people who speak unfiltered truth. I see it in senior citizens I know who are over age seventy that are in my family, in church, and pretty much anywhere I go. They often speak their truth and speak their mind unashamedly! I love that the freedom from childhood (how does the saying go, "*Out of the mouths of babes...*) has returned to set them free again in their old age. It's refreshingly hilarious, and painful, if you find yourself on the receiving end of that truth.

Youth, old age, and grief, why did it take so long for me to cut the tact and political correctness just to call a spade a spade? Why are people surprised when a quiet person decides just to call out the truth and then accuse them of "throwing shade?" Would one rather that a matter be veiled in gossip? In grief, youth and old age, or even in illness, one has no desire or inclination to waste time not being true to oneself, which sometimes means speaking the truth about others, and certainly the truth about one's self.

I once posted on Facebook that truth was the fuel of change. When we can look at ourselves, others, and our situations and speak and see the truth, where change needs to happen, we can identify and make the choice, with integrity, to change or not. And being able to move in integrity because you decided to see, hear, internalize, and act on the truth makes you an adult, for real. There is no cliché in the scripture from John 8:32, "If you continue in My Word you really are my disciples. You will know the truth, and the truth shall set you free." [HCSB] There is a special knowledge of the truth when you have decided to accept Jesus as your personal Savior. There is the world's truth and then there's God's truth. If you only got the world's truth, you wouldn't understand God's truth. But if you have God's truth, you can know and understand all truth that matters.

Who am I today and what is my identity? I have spent the first twenty years of my life with several labels and identities: Susie's grand, Vera's daughter, John's daughter, Professor, John Jr.'s sister; then I transitioned into the next twenty-two years as Noni's mom. I embrace all of these labels because of the love I have for the people who gave me them; though I hold only one label, Professor, the one my Grandpa Plenty gave me, was especially near and dear to my heart. That nickname was prophetic; neither he nor any of my grandmothers lived long enough to see me become a minister, teach, preach, coach, or counsel, but I love how God can speak a prophetic word into people for others, and when the potential is fulfilled in that person, it's pretty amazing.

Professor was the only label given to me that was just about me and who I am. Yes, I am known as Reverend Doctor, but without a pastorate or place at a college or university to teach, for me it feels purely academic, without any action behind it. This means so much to me at this point in life. Developmentally speaking, people in my stage of life are experiencing increased flexibility in family dynamics, as their children are maturing and looking for more independence, however, at the same time their parents start taking on a more dependent role. It's said to be the "sandwich" generation, where one takes care of adolescent and young adult children as well as their own parents. Despite this, one now has time to reconnect with the self, personally and professionally, and there are options and opportunities for change.

I find myself mothering my young adult child on a different level than most mothers of other twenty-two-year-old children. My child has completed her studies with honors, when she is not teaching music, she travels the world, touring , earning a wage and living her passion in song. With both of my parents now deceased, and my daughter's amazing life that she's carving out for herself, there is definitely a gaping hole in my life. There is a feeling of not having a covering, someone who will have your back if things go south in life. I think I'm not alone in having that feeling of protection that you've been used to from your parents. No person or parent is perfect, but what a blessing it's been to me to have parents, despite their flaws and mine, to love me and make me feel protected. Not everyone has that experience, which is important to remember. There is a feeling, particularly for me as a single person, as to who will care? Good parents have to love and care for their children! I heard someone say that they finally knew what it was like to become a grownup, at the death of their last parent. I think there is an air of truth to that statement; it's truly just you against the world. This doesn't diminish the reality of my large extended family of aunts, uncles, and a myriad of cousins, but not having them near in proximity adds to the loneliness. This is the reality we all will face at some point or another. That is why connection is so important. I've had a circle of close friends with me for decades; we don't see each other every day or even speak every day, but I know they have my back. I wouldn't mind expanding this circle; I need a tribe and a village to keep me sane. We weren't created for isolation, we were made for community.

So, who am I and where am going? I struggle for relevance and existence, so I won't be forgotten. Yes, I admit, I spent so many years in roles attached to others, that I hadn't completely carved out the natural role God had in mind for me. I struggle for relevance and existence because we are born to be relevant. there is a purpose and place for each and every one of us, but the wiles of the enemy, and circumstance can derail one's focus. Which is another reason to stay connected to the Creator and His guidebook. I know that in today's culture, the youth are celebrated and maybe even worshiped, but I believe that God made no mistakes in planning this space in the lives of adults as a means to get some of His greatest work and inspiration accomplished through His people. Old enough to get it done financially, wise enough to understand the effects on themselves and the world around them.

For me, this space in time has been one of questioning. I feel my parents had a different perspective in the loss of their mothers because they had each other and still had young children to focus on, to help them move through the grief more easily and to continue to move forward in life. It's really easy to feel lost. For a long time, I felt lost because a big part of who I was, was no longer here.

I submit to you that if you have experienced anything similar to what I have described, I certainly feel your pain. But I want to share with you that not only do I understand and feel your pain, I also know of someone who knows and understands, He is greater than your grief and your pain, God provides so many promises in His Word that can truly help us get through hard times. God walks ahead of us, and He knows what's coming next; He walks behind us because He has our backs; and He walks alongside us holding our right hand. He is our protection when we feel unprotected. He is a Father and a friend when we feel lonely. In those moments when we feel scared, God has and continues to reassure us, telling us, "Don't be afraid!" Why? Because God is here to help us! Psalm 121 says, " I lift my eyes toward the mountains, where will my help come from? My help comes from the Lord, the Maker of heaven and earth." [HCSB] NOW ISN'T THAT GOOD NEWS?

I had so many days and nights where nothing, including this promise, could console me, but even when I couldn't consciously tap into His presence, God never stopped holding my hand. God showed up in many ways, subtle ways, that sometimes I didn't recognize until I was in my reflecting moments. In my darkest days of grief, in the many days that I considered death as a relief for the overwhelming sadness I endured, I know my Lord was speaking into my spirit, "I am here to help you." God is still holding my hand, comforting me, and reassuring me of His presence.

Certainly, the grieving process is different for everyone, so unfortunately, I don't know how long it will hurt. I know an individual who has been grieving hard for years and treats the anniversary of their parents' death as if the death just happened. I still get teary-eyed about my parents on certain occasions, but I'm pretty sure they wouldn't want me to be paralyzed by the grief, engulfed by sadness. My guess is that they would want to be remembered with a smile and laughs, and I want that too.

Now, in this phase of my life, is where I actually have the time to explore and step into my identity. Who am I?

I am still learning and still exploring, getting reacquainted with my likes and dislikes. I'm reconnecting with one of the best people I know, me. I know I continue to love the warmer weather of summer like what is found in Caribbean beaches. I love taking long walks, being by the water. I love being with down-to-earth people like me, whom I can have great conversations with. I love to laugh. I love men, God-fearing men! I love it when a man knows how to take charge but gives his woman space to be herself. I love a man who knows how to be attentive to his woman and lets her know daily what she means to him; a man who does what he says and knows how to commit to his woman. I love good music, good food, and living life.

Who am I?
I am a woman who has found her voice and enjoys expressing herself-freely. My podcast, the *Your Success Personally Podcast*, something I thought would be totally outside of myself, has been such a wonderfully growing experience. I love exploring ideas of what success really means, talking to real people who have made success on their own terms, and sharing with the growing audience tips, tools, and ideas around the subject. It is an extension of me. I am using my voice because it needs to be heard; otherwise, God wouldn't have given me one. The same is true for you.

I know I don't like bullies and those who seek to hurt and destroy, those who'd rather cut corners than be willing to put in the required work. I don't like it when people don't take care of their homes and neighborhoods. I don't like it when people go out of their way to be mean or disrespectful, just because.

The key for me is to stay in tune with myself, my highs and my lows. I look to get things done, but I make a conscious effort to take care of me, stay connected to my feelings, take my pulse where I am now, and I do a lot less forecasting for the future. That might sound strange to some, but I spent a lot of time in my youth looking forward to the future, spending a lot of time living for the future instead of enjoying the moment. I've lived long enough to realize that I might have missed a lot of great moments in the present, because I wasn't in it, always thinking about the next moment. So, I pay attention to the now because I can sometimes run ahead of myself without taking time to smell the roses.

Who am I now?
I am a work in progress, and I'm working it. I don't pretend to have it all together, nor has this book been about proclaiming that I have arrived. I would say that my life right now is like the scripture found in Philippians 3:13-14, "Brothers, I do not consider myself to have taken hold of it. But one thing I do: forgetting what is behind and reaching forward to what is ahead, I pursue as my

goal the prize promised by God's heavenly call in Christ Jesus." [HCSB]

What this means for me, is that despite a life filled with mistakes of varying consequences, I am courageous enough to trust God and live the Word God inspired Paul to write. I'm not going backward; even when I feel like I don't want to go on, there is a higher call on my life than my feelings dictate. I press on because I've been called to do so. Even on the lowest days, and those days do come, there is a call, a goal, and a purpose on my life, and to stop short of my destiny, just won't cut it. There is joy in the journey, but whether or not I experience it, well, that's up to me—a matter of my perspective on any given day. I exist, I am relevant, and I am the pleasure of my God and my Lord and Savior Jesus Christ.

Scripture says in Psalm 139:14, "I will praise you because I have been remarkably and wondrously made. Your works are wondrous and I know this very well." [HCSB]

There was great care in making me, and whether you like it or not, I'm a marvelous creation of the Most High and I will no longer be distracted by the wiles of the enemy from doing what God has made me and called me to do. And so, it should be with you.

But what about you? Can you say you are tuned in and can rattle off a list, even if it is a short list of five things that make your heart sing and five things you would want to do away with in the world? There was a time that what I liked or disliked wasn't at the forefront of my consciousness. If you're anything like me; trying to conquer the world and being Supermom a day at a time, you are likely saving everyone else in their world and leaving your world barely attended to. It is a wonderful thing to be able to be that type of person in other people's lives; but as you continue to show up in a big way in everyone else's lives, somehow, without proper care and attention, you might notice your life, your goals and dreams diminishing. When your life has become more about the people you love and your service to them, and you can only find very few traces left of you, my advice to you, from experience, is to find balance.

Balance is the key to success in every area of your life. I don't mean balance by having equal time for all that you do, this may not be realistic, but a balance in giving more time to the project or goal at hand than the others, but **ALWAYS** factoring you (your needs, your wants, your identity) into your life. Will that always happen perfectly? No, so don't look for it to be that way. My hope is that you will **stay awake to you** at all times, even when you recognize that your needs are getting lost in the shuffle. Your well-being, spiritually, physically, mentally, emotionally, and socially, should be important enough that you can make the adjustments that will keep you whole while you save the world.

No matter what stage of life you're in, never be afraid of change. Our God is not a God of stagnation. Everything

He has made has gone through an evolutionary process and that includes us in all the ways that make us who we are. The difference between us and plants, other inanimate objects and animals is free will. If we choose to resist to change in our spiritual, mental, social, and emotional lives, we will miss out on God's great plan. The Bible says in Romans 12:2, "Do not be conformed to this age, but be transformed by the renewing of your mind, so that you may discern what is the good, pleasing, and perfect will of God."[HCSB]

Are you willing to grow and evolve as God has always meant for you to do? Not just for you to make a better world, but also a better you in the process.

# PRESENT PERIOD: INTO THE FUTURE

B ecause in this present period, I am more aware now than I ever was before, like it says in Psalm 90, I have to number my days.

Who knows the day or the hour? Not I.

I marked the beginning of this period as 2009 as the days were quickly coming to an end in 2015. At rock bottom, having been rejected in ministry early on and duped in my day job, I was at a crossroads. I couldn't go into a future period looking back at this one and find that nothing's changed. No, this had to be a period that catapulted me into another period in which I felt I had learned lessons and reached a few mountaintops.

I love the Psalm 90:12 scripture because it's so sobering. It really hits home for me. As I still mourn the death of my mom and as I grow older, I look at my life, and not everything is what I've hoped for. With Psalm 90:12, you cannot hide in ambiguity: the verse says what it says. I find that I come back to this whenever I feel I've lost my way. It wakes me up and focuses me on what I need to be doing. Let me preface that statement by saying, that as believers in Christ, we don't have to be *doing* much of anything, other than loving God with all our hearts, minds, and soul and loving one another. That is truly it. However, that love toward God and man is made manifest through the answering of one's calling.

So, where I end is where I began and where I will continue to be as long as God gives me breath. The rejection in my day job, as it turns out was a blessing in disguise. If I got that position that was taken from me, I would have been blind to the people whom I really was working with. People are who they are, and they continuously show us who they are over and over again. Deviousness showed itself quite clearly, and if I were to have been in that position, I would have clearly rebelled against that atmosphere. However, it took time for me to grieve and to see the options opened up ahead of me. I was also left naked before myself, emotionally, spiritually, and mentally, so I could see what was going on inside me. So much had been unresolved within me, that I had no clue about, until adversity struck. Some of my deepest fears and my deepest yearnings have been revealed in the death of opportunities that I thought would come to fruition.

Psalm 90 gives us a picture of why we should number our days…Verses 1–12 say:

> "Lord, you have been our refuge in every generation. Before the mountains were born, before you gave birth to the earth and the world, from eternity to eternity you are God. You return mankind to dust, saying, "Return, descendant of Adam." For

in your sight a thousand years are like yesterday that passes by, like a few hours of the night. You end their lives, they sleep. They are like grass that grows in the morning-in the morning it sprouts and grows; by evening it withers and dries up. For we are consumed by your anger; we are terrified by your wrath. You have set our unjust ways before you, our secret sins in the light of your presence. For all our days ebb away under your wrath; we end our years like a sigh. Our lives last seventy years or, eighty years. Even the best of them is struggle and sorrow; indeed, they pass quickly, and we fly away. Who understands the power of your anger? Your wrath matches the fear that is due you. Teach us to number our days carefully so that we may develop wisdom in our hearts."[HCSB]

When I think about my life, I've spent so many years living for and unto myself, but scripture tells us that kind of thinking and living is misguided because our God is at the center of this world and should be at the center of our world. He's in control and He's omnipotent. I cannot imagine what God thinks when we make our plans for this and that; does He laugh, or does He cry? We spend a lot of time doing all sorts of things; unfortunately, I can say with confidence that there isn't enough of us spending time seeking God's plan for our lives. We don't remember that the life we live is a gift in time, and then it is no more. God's day is a thousand years to our one say none of us have ever lived that long, and we never will. We act like we will live forever; we overlook that God sent His Son Jesus for our salvation and that He will come again for the victory. We forget that before the victory, the war will be waged, and for some, the decision has to be made: to live for Christ or die to sin. We act like God has gone blind to what we do, what we say, our motivations; so many of us are not on the same wavelength as God. We forget that God has set before us a certain number of years, and that's it. God puts in us the desire for Him, to teach us to number our days, to consider how we spend our time; what we do, why we do, and with whom we spend it, so that we can come to know the wisdom God has for us.

Maybe that's a bit heavy for you, but I would hope that you would consider that living without consideration and mindlessly, is not truly living. My hope is that we all, young and old, come to a consciousness of how we live every day; a consciousness and awareness to live on purpose every day. To desire to love every day; to use God-given gifts, to be kind, Christ-like in your lifestyle. To make an impact on someone or even on this world, for the better. I would love to see the whole world live to want to laugh more, to make a positive difference on others, to endeavor to make someone smile, just because.

Perhaps these are musings that don't necessarily suit you. This journey is one that is still evolving for me. I don't remember why I began writing this book, but I am glad that my mom knew of it and endorsed such an under-taking. I'm glad my dad always believed that I could do something like this, and I'm glad that God took me through so many twists and turns in this life, so I can offer this extension of me; it's a new child awaiting to be birthed.

Finally, the one thing that I'd like for anyone reading this to take away from, is that **insights can be gained in the hours and days of our lives**. I hope that I can change your perspective on life's journey; even when things do not work out the way you've planned. I want to encourage you not to give up, even when life's circumstances do not initially show how things will work out. I will say it again, God has us in mind at all times, He says so in Jeremiah 29:11 says, "For I know the plans I have for you-this is the Lord's declaration-'plans for your well-being, not for disaster, to give you a future and a hope." [HCSB]

I had many circumstances that were perceived in the moment as setbacks, but God has had a plan for my life that surpassed any negative circumstances. God always has had and continues to have my best interest, my welfare in mind despite what has happened to me. I have been given reason to have hope because my future is well in hand.

So, as the sun has risen on your life, despite how the morning went, no matter what the noonday had you work out and the afternoon light has revealed to you, I hope that you won't stop or give up on yourself or your dreams! I hope, too, that as you come to face the twilight of your life, you realize the future God still has for you!

# BIBLIOGRAPHY

Elwell, W. A., Baker Theological Dictionary of the Bible. Baker Academic, Ada, MI, 2001.

Hawthorne G. F., Reid, D. G., Martin, R. P., The Dictionary of Paul and His Letters. Intervarsity Press, Downers Grove, IL, 1993.

Issler, K., Wasting Time with God: A Christian Spirituality of Friendship with God. Intervarsity Press, Downers Grove, IL., 2001.

Rampersad, A., Roessel, D., The Collected Poems of Langston Hughes, Alfred A. Knopf, NY, NY 1994

Smith, G. T., Courage and Calling: Embracing Your God-Given Potential. IVP Books, Downers Grove, IL, 1999.

Spencer, A. B., Beyond the Curse: Women Called to Ministry. Baker Academic, Ada, MI 1989.

Whitlock, G., From Call to Service: The Making of a Minister. Westminster Press, Philadelphia PA, 1968.

# ABOUT THE AUTHOR

*"We can all create a sunset, but it takes someone special to create a new dawn."*

Anthony T. Hincks.

 Vanessa Guest is a native New Yorker. She attended CUNY/York College where she earned a Bachelor of Science in Business Administration and became a proud member of Alpha Kappa Alpha Sorority, Inc. Dr. Guest earned a Master of Divinity degree at NYACK/ Alliance Theological Seminary Nyack, NY. In June of 2010, Dr. Guest earned her doctorate in Christian Counseling from the Andersonville Theological Seminary. Dr. Guest received and accepted the call to the preaching ministry and was licensed on June 12, 2001 when she embarked on a ministry of preaching and teaching. Dr. Guest later received a Master of Arts degree from NYACK/Alliance Graduate School of Counseling, in New York.

Currently, Dr. Guest continues to serve as minister and leader of the counseling ministry at her church, and resident mental health counselor in a private practice.

She is a mom and recently launched a podcast called, the **Your Success Personally Podcast**, that focuses on conversations about and highlighting success, self-esteem, organizational skills, and other self-help topics.

Dr. Guest is saved, by the grace of God, and lives by this scripture: John 10:10, *"… I have come that they might have life, and that they might have it more abundantly."* NKJV

CPSIA information can be obtained
at www.ICGtesting.com
Printed in the USA
LVHW081443090721
692105LV00020BA/1249

WHEN YOU THINK YOU CAN'T COME BACK
FROM ALL THE WRONG TURNS IN LIFE

**NOTHING WASTED:
LESSONS LEARNED ALONG MY JOURNEY**

It is said that "hindsight is 20/20."

In this book, Rev. Dr. Vanessa Guest brings the reader insights on the less than perfect life to illuminate how God can bring one back on the path of His purpose!

If you ever thought that you couldn't recover from mistakes and raw deals handed to you in life-think again! With the backdrop of her less than perfect life, she uses to highlight the lessons learned from her life story to speak of the uncontrollable and the unexpected, the devastation and the downturns, the highs and bright spots life can bring. Dr. Guest shows us how faith in God and reliance on. His Word to highlight how foundational lessons and that sometimes, even when God allows pain and heartbreak to come into your life, nothing is ever lost, ***nothing is truly wasted***; when God has a vision and plan for your life!

*"We can all create a sunset, but it takes someone special to create a new dawn."*
Anthony T. Hincks.

**Vanessa Guest** is a native New Yorker. She attended CUNY/York College where she earned a Bachelor of Science in Business Administration and became a proud member of Alpha Kappa Alpha Sorority, Inc. Dr. Guest earned a Master of Divinity degree at NYACK/ Alliance Theological Seminary Nyack, NY. In June of 2010, Dr. Guest earned her doctorate in Christian Counseling from the Andersonville Theological Seminary. Dr. Guest received and accepted the call to the preaching ministry and was licensed on June 12, 2001 when she

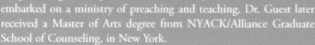

embarked on a ministry of preaching and teaching. Dr. Guest later received a Master of Arts degree from NYACK/Alliance Graduate School of Counseling, in New York.

Currently, Dr. Guest continues to serve as minister and leader of the counseling ministry at her church, and resident mental health counselor in a private practice.

She is a mom and recently launched a podcast called, the <u>Your Success Personally Podcast</u>, that focuses on conversations about and highlighting success, self-esteem, organizational skills, and other self-help topics.

 Dr. Guest is saved, by the grace of God, and lives by this scripture: John 10:10, "… I have come that they might have life, and that they might have it more abundantly." NKJV

ISBN 978-1-6628-1433-4
90000

Xulon PRESS

9 781662 814334